T0275107

Seeing Green

Seeing Green

HOW TO SAVE THE PLANET AND PROFIT FROM SUSTAINABILITY

ANGEL LANCE

Forbes | Books

Published by Forbes Books, Charleston, South Carolina.
Member of Advantage Media.

Forbes Books is a registered trademark, and the Forbes Books colophon is a trademark of Forbes Media, LLC.

Printed in the United States of America.

10 9 8 7 6 5 4 3 2 1

ISBN: 979-8-88750-487-2 (Paperback)
ISBN: 979-8-88750-440-7 (Hardcover)
ISBN: 979-8-88750-441-4 (eBook)

Library of Congress Control Number: 2023914877

Cover design by David Taylor.
Layout design by Lance Buckley.

This custom publication is intended to provide accurate information and the opinions of the author in regard to the subject matter covered. It is sold with the understanding that the publisher, Forbes Books, is not engaged in rendering legal, financial, or professional services of any kind. If legal advice or other expert assistance is required, the reader is advised to seek the services of a competent professional.

In order to maintain anonymity, in some instances names of individuals may have been changed, as well as some identifying characteristics and details such as physical properties, occupations, and places of residence. All ideas, opinions, and memories are the author's own, and while there is always a chance this does not align with other living memories, it is not the author's intent to misremember or disparage any individual or entity mentioned herein.

Since 1917, Forbes has remained steadfast in its mission to serve as the defining voice of entrepreneurial capitalism. Forbes Books, launched in 2016 through a partnership with Advantage Media, furthers that aim by helping business and thought leaders bring their stories, passion, and knowledge to the forefront in custom books. Opinions expressed by Forbes Books authors are their own. To be considered for publication, please visit **books.Forbes.com**.

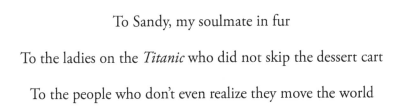

To Sandy, my soulmate in fur

To the ladies on the *Titanic* who did not skip the dessert cart

To the people who don't even realize they move the world

CONTENTS

FOREWORD

This is not a textbook and mostly not a cookbook. This book is sharing my understanding of the world based on my personal experience, and as I have not stopped experiencing life, I get more knowledge and my opinions shift. Even since this book has been written, my thoughts on many of these topics have evolved. Ultimately the intent of the stories I share here is to spark conversation and more thought on the matter of the environment and humanity's place in it. I want to bring new people to the table in these conversations, people who haven't traditionally realized their role in this space. More ideas and more approaches will be the only thing that shifts our relationship with each other and the planet.

If this book pisses you off—in whole or in part—don't just point out the problems, put forward your alternative solutions, too. Ultimately what matters is that we are all part of this important conversation and that we are all working towards solutions from many different lenses.

— Angel

Introduction

So, human-caused climate change is a thing. It is going to have impacts on the ecosystems of earth and human society. Let me clearly state that the planet will be fine, in the sense that it will continue regardless of what's going on with the living things on it—that's the good news. Human society, maybe not so much—that's the bad news. A stable climate is important for a stable society.

But we are not alone. In addition to the impacts of climate change, we are also facing a biodiversity crisis that climate change will make worse. In the 3.7 billion years of history of life on earth, there have been mass extinction events five times before, making this earth's sixth mass extinction.

My scientist friend, who I will call Dr. Tatiana Smith (a.k.a. Spock, a.k.a. Saucy Smith), is an ecologist with over two decades of experience. She explains that a mass extinction event is when a large number of species go extinct over a very short (geologically speaking) period of time. This sounds like the plot point of many apocalyptic thriller movies.

The sixth of anything might make it seem like par for the course. However, there are a couple of things we may want to consider in regard to the current mass extinction. The first is that it likely won't fare well for humans. The other is that this mass extinction is different from all those that came previously. The current mass extinction event is the only one ever caused by a single species, humans (an award we really don't want to receive), a species that has only been around about two hundred thousand to three hundred thousand years.[1] For reference, the previous mass extinction wiped out the dinosaurs (no fault of their own), who were on earth for 165 million years, and most humans acknowledge that they were pretty cool—I mean, we're still putting them on T-shirts and using them as star characters of morning cartoons and blockbuster films.

DR. TATIANA SMITH'S UNSOLICITED SCIENCE LESSON

"The comparison between human existence and the dinosaur existence is problematic. Humans are a single species, dinosaurs were two orders (a classification with hundreds of species that evolved, existed, and went extinct at different times). It would be more appropriate to compare the timeline of primates to the timeline of dinosaurs—primates have been around for roughly 66 to 85 million years, depending on which researcher you ask."

(You see? Spock)

Again, the good news is that the planet will be fine. Limiting climate change is about preserving the quality of our life. If humans get wiped out, as we would deserve having caused the situation, the earth will recover (over millions of years), revitalize, and become Eden again, and the surviving cockroaches and crocodiles will evolve into something amazing.

Let me also clearly state that I think the human race is a cancer on the earth. I cannot wait until Thanos comes to extinguish half of us, which probably makes it seem like I am not the best candidate to write this book. But I put a lot of effort into taking care of the cancer of the

---

1   Brian Handwerk, "An Evolutionary Timeline of Homo Sapiens," Smithsonian.com, February 2, 2021, accessed February 1, 2023, https://www.smithsonianmag.com/science-nature/essential-timeline-understanding-evolution-homo-sapiens-180976807/.

SOME OTHER PLEASURABLE THINGS ABOUT LIFE

- Tacos
- French cheese
- A Parisian café
- Gardening and harvesting your own food
- Flannel sheets
- A nongreasy massage
- Great champaign
- A beautiful sunrise/sunset
- Swimming in clear water
- Touching a wild animal because it trusts you
- Reading beachside
- Italian coffee bars
- Hiking without a plan but with a picnic
- Sequin pants
- House dinner parties
- Music and singing
- Dancing while making dinner

earth. And luckily for that cancer, I do my best work out of spite.

Also, I am an entrepreneur, and therefore I like imagining possibilities and solving problems. As part of the human race—all flaws that make me part of that cancer, in fact, I understand the part of human nature that is driving us toward destruction. And I love that nature. I love to taste and smell and see. I like wine, good food, and beautiful things, as well as a deep hot bath, scenery, and sex. I love the experience of life and existence, and I would like to revel in the joy of life for as long as possible. After all, what is the point of preserving life if we can't enjoy it?

So don't worry. This isn't one of those books that's going to tell you to abandon everything that gives you pleasure in the name of addressing climate change. Quite the contrary, this book is about allowing ourselves, as humans, the pleasures of life and preserving their possibilities.

———

Like most of my life's pathways, the one that carved its way to this place of author was very unintentional. I did not set out to embark on

4

outreach or to become a climate activist or an educator. I begrudgingly despise all these roles, although I am committed to them for now.

I grew up in a poor and violent household. (Don't worry, I'm not about to tell you my sob story.) The reason that matters is that it taught me to be a survivor. I'm resourceful, and that resourcefulness has served me well. It is the reason why my businesses and other pursuits are successful. Also, I tend to compensate for the fact that no one provided for me when I was a child with a compulsion to care for things and people now (even things and people who annoy me).

I first came to environmentalism in a very personal and nominal way. At some point, I realized that I feel better about myself when I'm not destroying the place where I live. But like everyone else, I still want to fly to Italy every year and eat steak. I love the freedom of being alive, and I don't like the existing all-or-nothing solutions. The entrepreneur in me began to ask, "What's possible? How do I do and get all the things I want and feel good about it (in a not-killing-the-planet sort of way)?" And because I'm an entrepreneur and own multiple companies, my concern is also: "What will make money?"

I began to think about environmental consciousness in terms of an equitable transaction. This started as small, personal initiatives (recycling, composting, buying reusable rather than disposable items) to reduce my debt to the environment. (I realize that these actions won't make a big dent in climate change, but they will minorly make it less bad.) Then I started to consider ways to export my environmental sensibility and found different ways that I could capitalize on my business and my business sense to take an ecological stance. I want to widen the frame around the ecological economy so that people don't only think "sweaty hippie." I want to make participation in the ecological economy pragmatic for the everyday person and advantageous for the businessperson.

I first started doing this at my consulting business, Motive Power. So long as we were advising other companies, I decided that we should be advising them with a slant (ours is a very steep slope) toward ESG (Environmental Social Governance) compliance, sustainability, and environmental awareness—things that are both good for the environment and also essential to any company's public relations campaign and survival in the market. I continued this mission in my other businesses, like 10/6 Professional Services, and later established a nonprofit called the Gulch Environmental Foundation, which actually creates and promotes atmospheric carbon sequestration initiatives. I also founded an organization called the National Public Utility Council (NPUC) that works with utility companies to get to net-zero carbon dioxide emissions. Through my environmental mission, I work with people in various businesses who in turn work with varied communities with wildly diverse perspectives on climate change and ESG-related initiatives in general. And all these things are good for my business. For every business, thinking of things through an environmental lens is a triple win that not only addresses issues around climate change but also makes businesses more profitable and strategically positioned in the emerging economy.

I also now, through my nonprofit, own a farm (because it fits my mission, and driving a tractor makes me feel cool), but you don't need to take it this far. Becoming environmentally conscious is not expensive or difficult. You don't need to make radical changes. Nothing I did is amazing. Everyone can do this, and I'm going to show you how.

This is not a kid-gloves, spiritual-self-help, granola-will-save-the-world kind of book (not that there's anything wrong with that, but see my favorite granola recipe on the next page if that's what you're into). Nor is this a doomsday, apocalyptic, let's-all-build-bunkers-and-form-armed-posses kind of book (although again, to each his/her own).

This is a practical, take-action, quit-whining-and-roll-up-your-sleeves, get-educated, make-a-plan, and dig-in kind of book. We can do this. Let's get started.

ANGEL'S FAVORITE GRANOLA RECIPE

Easy Energy Balls

Prep Time: 15 minutes | Cook Time: 0 minutes | Yield: 20 1x

This peanut butter energy balls recipe is the best easy snack! Healthy oatmeal balls pack protein and fiber into tasty bites.

Ingredients

- 2 cups Old-Fashioned rolled oats
- 1/2 cup creamy peanut butter (no sugar added, or any nut butter or sunflower butter for nut free)
- 1/3 cup honey (or agave syrup for vegan)
- 1/4 teaspoon kosher salt
- 1/4 teaspoon cinnamon
- 1/4 cup vanilla or chocolate protein powder (optional)
- 3 tablespoons mini chocolate chips

Instructions

Mix all ingredients together in a bowl. Freeze the bowl for 5 minutes.

Roll the dough into 20 small balls, pressing the dough together with your hands. We used a 1 1/2-inch cookie scoop (#40) to make uniform balls. You can also make smaller balls if desired. (If the texture of your nut butter makes the dough very dry, add a little more honey or a few tablespoons milk of choice until you can press it together into a ball shape.) Refrigerate for up to 2 weeks. Enjoy! [2]

---

2   Sonja Overhiser, (2022, July 29), *Easy energy balls*, A Couple Cooks, https://www. acouplecooks.com/energy-balls/.

In addition to telling the story of my mission to get my companies and others to net-zero carbon dioxide emissions, my trials and triumphs as a farmer in Oklahoma, and important nonfactual information about dinosaurs, this book will offer tips to various users, in the below three tiers, on how to get started based on the investment that you are willing and able to make. Of course, the more you put into it, the more you will get out of it. Many of you, like me, may occupy more than one or even all of these tiers.

The following tiers offer ways for participants to get a triple win and multiple paybacks on their investments. But all of them require that you take action to make that initial investment. This means you're probably going to need to put the book down eventually and get off your couch—start psyching yourself up.

Tier 1: The Savvy At-Home Composter

No matter what tier you ultimately seek, this is a great place to start. At home, work, and in my daily life, I am a savvy composter. The Savvy Composter is a person willing to invest a small amount of money and time into taking environmental actions at home or in the office on his/her own. This has the smallest impact on the overall environment but can have huge impacts on your personal life, including reducing living expenses, making you feel good about yourself, and providing you with fresh veggies.

Tier 2: The CEO Environmental Powerhouse

Through the multiple companies that I run, I am also a CEO Environmental Powerhouse. This tier is for CEOs, entrepreneurs, business leaders, and others in leadership or managerial positions willing to transform their companies to be ESG compliant, participate in environmental discussions, and invest in community initiatives. These actions have a great impact on your institution's carbon dioxide emissions, have the potential to influence the awareness and behavior of a wider community, and can also glean rewards for your businesses in terms of improving public relations, employee and client retention, and increasing overall profits.

Tier 3: The Big Cheese World Changer

This is for the Warren Buffct business magnates, investors, leaders within government, and philanthropists who oversee multiple companies or make impacts across multiple companies, markets, and/or regions and who are willing to make large investments of time and resources to transform companies and direct industries and public policies to be more ESG compliant through efforts that include organizing, collaborating, influencing, promoting, and funding. These actions have the wide ranging most impact on carbon dioxide emissions and also glean the greatest rewards in terms of growth across companies, overall profit, and improved public relations not only for individual brands but also for entire sectors and government initiatives. Through the creation of an organization called the NPUC (National Public Utilities Council) that unites utilities across the country to work toward decarbonization in the energy industry, I have become a Big Cheese World Changer impacting work infrastructure.

ACCORDING TO OUR WEBSITE

"The National Public Utilities Council (NPUC) is a leading research organization dedicated to driving progress in the decarbonization of power generation."[3]

In the San Francisco Bay Area, where I live, and everywhere, we are already experiencing climate change. That can no longer be prevented. But we are all collectively in charge of how bad things will get, and we are the last generation that will have the opportunity to prevent climate change from reaching catastrophic tipping points. We can either throw up our hands and have the last biggest tailgate party in history while we wait for the apocalypse, or we can take action. I think we have an obligation to keep the world an inhabitable place for our children. And I think we have the agency, intelligence, and power to do so if we are properly motivated. The problem is big, but humans have solved big problems in the past. We can make these choices as individuals by taking action in one or all of the above three tiers: changing our lifestyle, changing the way we conduct business, and adopting as a global community regulations and creating standards for countries and industries. Everything matters now. All hands on deck.

A RAY OF SUNSHINE/HOPIUM

The Conference of Parties (COP) is an annual meeting of the world's governments established in 1995. The COP's goal is to work collaboratively to solve climate change. They review the emissions and goals of participating organizations, assess the effects of different actions, and propose solutions. The Paris Climate Agreement was one such proposal.

---

3   National Public Utilities Council, "Decarbonization report. Motive Power," April 18, 2023, https://www.motive-power.com/national-public-utilities-council/.

PART 1

The Big Footprint

CHAPTER 1

How 'Bout This Weather

The Weather Is No Longer a Casual Conversation Starter

It used to be that the weather was the go-to subject of inert conversation. It was polite, boring, and it allowed everyone to participate in uncontentious ways. It was the bland side dish of discussions—mashed potatoes, corn, bread roll. Now the weather is exciting, energizing our chitchat—not only the steak but also the topic of the forum at which dinner is being served.

The weather has become so puzzling and dynamic that it takes center stage. It can no longer be ignored or pushed to the background. The good news is that it remains a good, uncontentious, go-to conversation topic because people are so preoccupied with surviving and dealing with weather events that they don't have time to debate whether or not climate change exists.

The words "off-the-charts," "unprecedented," and "record-breaking" are now standard vocabulary for meteorologists on the nightly news, and stories of weather catastrophes—floods, hurricanes, tornadoes, droughts, heat waves that kill dozens or hundreds of people and causing incalculable damages—are such regular fare that the news shows have developed special little introductory tunes and icons. News broadcasts now have an ever-performing platform of sensational titles to work from complete with new and more explosive nomenclature that make the news sound like a Marvel movie: "rain bombs," "fire cyclones," "atmospheric rivers," and the ever-chilling "polar vortex." It is now the days of calm weather that are truly unexpected.

As I am writing this, there are smoke-free skies in California. Ten years ago, I would have thought nothing of clear skies, but today, they are unusual this time of year. Lately it has been rare to look up and see blue, or even to be able to go outside and take a deep breath in the fall. The skies have routinely been filled with dark, choking smoke.

AN OPENING SCENE FOR A MARVEL-STYLE ACTION MOVIE ABOUT CLIMATE CHANGE

Over darkness, we hear the voice or a narrator (hopefully played by Morgan Freeman or James Earl Jones).

Narrator: In an unrecognizable world, will we recognize the solutions in time?

The Scene Unfolds: *People carry belongings and children as they stream out of devastated areas, by boat, by plane, on buses, in cars, and on foot.*

A local newscaster watches from the temporary safety of a news room.

Newscaster: This is an image of people escaping the pending deluge of environmental events sinking their communities. Mega storms are making their ways across the country, possibly next hitting my neighborhood or yours. Channel 6 will keep a careful eye on this scene as it unfolds.

The voice of the narrator returns as we watch people drag themselves, their families, and everything they can carry away from environmental chaos.

Narrator: In a planet bombarded by one devastating natural disaster after another, three communities of people take action to make change: The Savvy At-Home Composter, The CEO Environmental Powerhouse, and The Big Cheese World Changer.

Dr. Tatiana tells me that fall has always been wildfire season on the West Coast (fire is a vital and natural part of our Mediterranean eco-systems here). However, the wildfires that are happening now are not occurring as they naturally have historically—they are not healthy, but they are natural disasters. A century of fire suppression combined with stressed vegetation due to climate change–induced drought have led to drastically larger and more intense wildfires. Few words better describe the feeling of living in California during our recent wildfire seasons than "apocalyptic."

A NOTE FROM DR. TATIANA

It's important to refer to this condition as "climate change" instead of "global warming." The term "climate change" captures that the impact's beyond just warming. This terminology has recently shifted further to "climate crisis" to highlight the magnitude of the issue: it is no longer merely change.

Photos taken of my neighborhood during heavy smoke days look like backgrounds for a Marvel movie poster. The entire sky, clouded by smoke, is flushed red as though itself is on fire. It is like looking at the world through orange-tinted glasses. Not only that but the skies are generally darker. Morning comes later; night comes earlier. And in between the diffused daylight looks like the world has stopped in a perpetual state of dawn or dusk.

This doesn't feel natural. Your body freaks out. You can't sleep and never feel fully awake. On a physiological level, you don't know if it is day or night. And if you think you're confused, you should get a load of the animals who don't know when to make noise, or burrow, or feed. Then there is the smell of char that saturates your skin, soaks through walls, and imbeds itself in the fibers of your clothes, your blankets, your pillows, the follicles of hair in your nose.

Those are the changes you can observe with your physical senses and measure with scientific gadgets. What is more difficult to name are your emotional and psychological responses, the communal sense that the world just isn't right, the weird energy (to use the lingo)—a sort of innate feeling rooted in a deep human survival instinct. That general feeling of unease manifests as anxiety, dread, and fear that builds to become as consuming as the fire.

There are now weeks in California when no one can concentrate. It is reminiscent of the feeling I had when rioting in the streets in LA was taking place close to my home, but not right at my doorstep—I'm not actually in it, but it's close or impending, and it leaves me feeling so uncertain about the immediate future that I just can't bring myself to care about things like the dishes or the latest crisis at work.

A NOTE FROM DR. TATIANIA

The AQI is a federal government system for reporting air quality supported by the EPA (Environmental Protection Agency), which has a higher quality data source for air quality than Purple Air, but a more limited number of sensors. You can access their site here: https://www.airnow.gov/.

Purple Air is a private company that uses sensors that people maintain in their homes, which means they have better coverage, but the quality of those sensors is not controlled. Both have pros and cons. You can see the official government data here: https://fire.airnow.gov/.

The wildfires for the past many fall seasons have lasted for days or weeks—without an end in sight. During wildfire season (because now we no longer call it "fall"), I check a website called Purple Air that provides a real-time Air Quality Index (AQI) map of the entire country. Purple Air labels local air qualities on a spectrum that measures particle pollution moving from 0–50 (satisfactory, posing no risk) to >300 (emergency conditions warning that everyone's health will likely be affected with a twenty-four-hour exposure). When the conditions grow worse, I find myself checking the site morning and night, then hourly.

"All but Three of the Top 20 Largest Wildfires Have Occurred Since 2000, with 5 of These Large and Damaging Wildfires Occurring Just This Year," [4]

During wildfire season, the focus of conversation for most Californians is air quality (interrupted by polite small talk about politics, education, work, and other things that no longer seem relevant). Often, because we are able to do so, my employees and I work from home and meet via video conference calls. We spend the first half of our meetings talking about weather conditions, the AQI, and reporting on everything we are seeing and doing to

---

4   Cal Fire, "All but Three of the Top 20 Largest #Wildfires Have Occurred Since 2000, with 5 of These Large and Damaging Wildfires Occurring Just This Year," Facebook, October 1, 2020, https://www.facebook.com/CALFIRE/photos/a.157450722389/1015 8753820557390/.

manage the effects of the air pollution—imagine a sewing circle where apocalyptic trends are the main gossip. The nightly news warns people to limit outdoor activity or discontinue it altogether if they have preexisting conditions. The news also reports damage to property, evacuations, injuries, deaths. The hospitals are filling up with patients whose breathing is impaired. Only recently has the news begun to associate these emergencies with climate change.

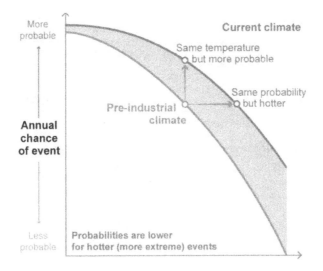

"Regional trends in extreme events in the IPCC 2021 report. Changes in climate result in changes in the magnitude and probability of extremes."[5]

So far human beings generally interact with climate change by reacting to the effects. People are responding as best they can—something that is discernibly separated by the haves and have-nots, as financial resources often determine how effectively you can buffer

5   V. Masson-Delmotte & P. Zhai, "Regional trends in extreme events in the IPCC 2021 report. Changes in climate result in changes in the magnitude and probability of extremes," World Meteorological Organization, https://public.wmo.int/en/resources/ bulletin/regional-trends-extreme-events-ipcc-2021-report.

yourself from these elements. People who have to physically go to work wrap kerchiefs around their mouths, stuff eye drops in their pockets, and go to work. People who can stay home fortify their houses. Lines form around the block at Costco to buy the last air purifiers. Their filters clog in days. Replacements sell out. The HVAC people are overwhelmed and triple their prices to meet demand. Only wealthy people can afford clean air. In this way, air becomes a resource for which people compete.

I am fortunate to have a beach house that I covet in a new way during wildfire season: a place to breathe better. People with means, but without second homes, book AirBnbs in places with clear air that year and drive away. But some years there is no escape. The fires have been so bad that the people feel the effects in Oklahoma, Minneapolis, and even New York as smoke wafts from western states across the country. This really highlights that although wealth can buffer people initially, it will not do so indefinitely. This is something that will impact everyone and everywhere in some way.

POTENTIAL AIRBNB AD

Cozy apocalyptic escape! Great locations (underground bunker or orbiting the moon). Includes filtered oxygen, chemically cleaned water, and dehydrated foods that can be stored for up to 25 years. BYOB. Sorry, no pets, kids, or smoking.

Wildfires in the western states are not an isolated disaster. There are more and more climate change-related disasters every week. We run through the alphabet of tropical storms and need to start with *A* again, name more seasons for other weather events (tornado season, hurricane season, flood season), and come to expect to see our newscasters standing knee-deep in water, pummeled by wind that no hairspray can deter and dressed in hard hats and life jackets as they interview orange-jacketed FEMA representatives. We are now seeing drought levels in some regions that we haven't seen since the US began keeping records in the 1800s.[6]

By the time this book is published, any records that I document here will already be outdated. And this trend is global. The latest Intergovernmental Panel on Climate Change (IPCC) report showed that climate change is affecting every inhabited region across the globe. Our language is adapting accordingly, transitioning from "climate change" to "climate crisis."[7]

Out of Sight

There are all kinds of reasons why people do not take action to limit climate change. First, flaws in human nature make us reactive rather than proactive. Along with this, people have selective memories. In the moments when we are actively dealing with the effects of climate change, we are doing just that—responding in immediate ways to make our lives more livable, trying not to melt in record-breaking heat waves, staying indoors to avoid weather, buying air purifiers so that we can breathe, and flying the coop for clearer skies. We don't make time to think about the larger causes or invest in making the big changes that could correct or mitigate the root problem. And once the effects are over, we have an out-of-sight-out-of-mind mentality—we forget how bad it is, tell ourselves it won't happen again, and occupy our minds with the latest scandal on social media.

---

6   Guardian News and Media, "Megadrought in the American South-West: A Climate Disaster Unseen in 1,200 Years," *The Guardian*, September 12, 2022, accessed April 17, 2023, https://www.theguardian.com/environment/2022/sep/12/us-west-megadrought-climate-disaster.

7   Nick Reimer, "Climate Change" or "Climate Crisis" – What's the Right Lingo? Clean Energy Wire, September 19, 2019, accessed January 17, 2023, https://www.cleanenergy-wire.org/blog/climate-change-or-climate-crisis-whats-right-lingo.

But this ability of humans to dismiss what is not right in front of them is broad and remarkable. Not only can we forget our own past experiences, but we can also ignore present experiences going on far away. Watching an unseasonable typhoon in Asia or another hundred-year flood ravishing Europe this decade feels like fiction as the narrative unfolds alongside the latest crime shows we're binging.

It just doesn't seem real, or not like our reality anyway. The future, also, does not seem like it will be our reality, although predictions continue to come true and continue to be made. We forget the devastating effects of natural disasters that we live through, separate ourselves from any obvious natural disaster going on elsewhere, disbelieve the predictions about the future, and ignore the smaller but noticeable ways that climate change makes impacts on our everyday lives.

In addition, the effects of climate change are not immediate, like touching a hot stove. Instead, it is like charging something on a credit card for which you won't get the bill until the end of the month or looking at the night sky and seeing the light from stars that burned tens of thousands or millions of years ago. The climate changes that we are feeling today are due to actions we took about

DECARBONIZATION REPORT

In December 2022, Motive Power finished our Annual Utility and Decarbonization Report, and we have carefully scheduled the release date. What I've learned is that no one cares about climate change from late spring into late summer. It's the sweet spot before hurricane and wildfire season, after the gloom of winter when people are realizing their neighborhood lakes no longer freeze over. In order for people to care enough to read the report, the world needs to feel apocalyptic now.

twenty to thirty years ago[8] because it takes that long for the earth to heat up to the level the greenhouses gases dictate. (Think of the oceans, which make up around 70 percent of the earth's surface, as a pot of water set to boil. It takes a while for that water to heat up to match the temperature of the heat under the pot. It won't be ready for the pasta until the next generation is cooking in the kitchen.) All of this contributes to a fracture between what we logically know to be true and what we feel to be true. It feels like this just can't be happening.

A Little Education: Remember Your Elementary School Science Class

Learning about climate change has made me aware of the many gaps in people's general science knowledge, including my own. I once had someone ask me if I would ever drink anything radioactive. My immediate thought was that anything to do with radioactivity is definitely bad, and I don't want anything to do with it. I held a common misconception of what radioactive means.

Radioactivity is a process of decay. Plants absorb this radioactivity in the ground through their roots and in the air through photosynthesis. Animals, in turn, eat these plants. This means that all organic life on earth has a radioactive signature. Radioactive material is harmful to humans and all life, but small amounts are natural and manageable. If your wine is not radioactive, that means it is made of something unnatural that you definitely don't want in your body. As always, reality is more nuanced than our initial impressions.

---

8   Owen Mulhern, "The Time Lag of Climate Change," Earth.org, December 16, 2020, accessed April 17, 2023, https://earth.org/data_visualization/the-time-lag-of-climate-change.

Carbon dioxide (CO2) similarly gets a bad rap. We think of it as a noxious poison choking away our oxygen. But carbon is the main building block of life; without it, most things that we care about on earth, including the human race, would not be here. Remember that terrarium you built in third grade that made the classroom smell a little weird for a few weeks? The gist of the lesson was that everything in the ecosystem feeds something else, and the process of decay enables growth. That experiment contains essentially everything you need to know about how ecosystems work to grow plants, convert carbon dioxide into oxygen, and help living organisms thrive. The week you built the terrarium, one of your spelling words was likely *photosynthesis*, or the process by which plants absorb carbon dioxide from the air and combine it with water (H2O) to create the glucose they need to grow (essentially their food). This process is fueled by energy from the sun. Oxygen is produced as a by-product, (plant waste, or shit essentially) and is released into the atmosphere. People and other animals then breathe oxygen and exhale carbon dioxide. Some of your other spelling words from that week were likely *cycle, interdependence, interrelationships,* and *symbiosis.* So long as you left your terrarium in the sunlight, it was self-sustaining for the rest of the school year, recycling its own water and carbon dioxide.

The problem is that since the industrial revolution, humans have been giving a one-two punch to this natural cycle: both moving expo-

A NOTE FROM DR. TATIANA

People are apprehensive about terms often because they misunderstand them or don't understand them at all. Try asking someone if she is worried about consuming dihydrogen monoxide. Most people will be concerned about the unfamiliar chemical term. Dihydrogen monoxide is the name for a water molecule.

nential amounts of carbon dioxide into the air from the fossil fuels and also killing the plants (think deforestation) that store and convert carbon dioxide into oxygen and food. According to the World Economic Forum, since 1900 we have lost over one billion hectares of forest.[9] These forests have been harvested for wood, cleared for agriculture, devastated by wildfire, or diminished by changing climate regimes. The loss of these forests not only means that we remove them from the photosynthesis process, but killing the trees also releases the carbon dioxide that they store. The loss of tropical forests alone has created carbon dioxide emissions that, if ranked in comparison to the overall annual emissions of countries, would rank third in overall emissions[10] behind the top two carbon dioxide–producing nations: the United States and

A NOTE FROM DR. TATIANA

The word shit is completely unscientific and inaccurate. There are many kinds of waste, and this particular kind is nothing at all like excrement. This would be a metabolic by-product, like the carbon dioxide we breathe out, not unassimilated biomass—what shit is made out of.

China. This is not only due to the loss of the plants but also the loss of living microbes in those soils made possible by those forests—also carbon based. Nearly a billion metric tons[11] of carbon dioxide have been released from that soil alone. The good news is that also means there is room within those soils to sequester that carbon dioxide again.

9   "Here's How the Earth's Forests Have Changed since the Last Ice Age," *World Economic Forum*, April 7, 2022, https://www.weforum.org/agenda/2022/04/forests-ice-age/.

10   "Chart of the Day: What If Deforestation Were a Country," *World Economic Forum*, November 22, 2018, https://www.weforum.org/agenda/2018/11/chart-of-the-day-what-if-deforestation-were-a-country/.

11   "Land degradation also reduces carbon fixation since above and below ground biomass is compromised. In the period 1981–2003 this led to a loss of nearly a billion tonnes of carbon" (Bai et al. 2008), http://www.fao.org/resources/infographics/infographics-details/en/c/340783/.

MORE NEW VOCABULARY

According to the Oxford English Dictionary, tipping point is the threshold at which a series of small changes build to cause a significant (and in the case of climate change, often irreversible and accelerating) change.[12]

Tipping point used in a sentence: It's really important that humans get their shit together and act fast so that we don't keep triggering these damn tipping points.

Not included in your third-grade lesson on ecosystems was likely fossil fuels, the large pools of carbon dioxide created by prehistoric plants and animals from millions of years ago (long before there were dinosaurs) and stored underground mostly as coal, oil, and natural gas (that together make up about 15 percent of earth's carbon). When we burn fossil fuels, we take carbon stored as fossil fuels and convert them into atmospheric carbon, moving them into the atmospheric pool. Once transferred, we can't put them back into the fossil fuel pool. It's like combining ingredients to make a batch of cookies. When the dough is mixed, you can't get the eggs or flour back. And in terms of carbon dioxide, we are overexuberant bakers, seeming to have forgotten that our cookie jar is only so big. However, rather than just making you fat, an overabundance of carbon dioxide upsets natural cycles and threatens civilization on earth as we know it.

You probably didn't tackle greenhouse gas until high school biology. Like radioactive particles and carbon dioxide, this is another misunderstood element that frequently gets a bad rap.

---

12   *Tipping Point.* Oxford Reference. (n.d.). https://www.oxfordreference.com/display/10.1093/oi/authority.20110803104719110;jsessionid=F14AA5F4800A4F432F686A8A97AFA3D5.

Like carbon dioxide, greenhouse gases themselves are not bad; they are critical to making the earth habitable. The greenhouse effect is the process by which energy from the sun warms the earth's atmosphere. Light from the sun passes through our atmosphere pretty readily and warms the surface of the earth. After hitting the earth, that energy reflects back up. Greenhouse gases act like the glass panels on the top of a greenhouse; they allow that light energy to pass in but do not as easily allow it to pass out. Some of that energy is absorbed into the atmosphere, warming it and heating the air. Without these greenhouse gases creating this greenhouse effect, all the heat that hits the earth would escape back into space, and the average temperature of the earth would be too cold for humans, and most other living organisms, to survive. Our old friend carbon dioxide and methane are two of the most important greenhouse gases. Again, the problem is not greenhouse gases themselves, but the increased volume—we have added way too much in a short period of time. Continuing to add more of these gases is like building thicker and thicker layers of glass on the greenhouse.

FACTS FOR THE ADVANCED/OVERACHIEVERS

Your third-grade lesson also disregarded the world's oceans, which are the largest storage of CO_2 on earth, holding more than nineteen times the amount of CO_2 held in the land biosphere.[13]

---

13   Christopher L. Sabine, "Carbon Dioxide in the Ocean and Atmosphere," Water Encyclopedia, http://www.waterencyclopedia.com/Bi-Ca/Carbon-Dioxide-in-the-Ocean-and-Atmosphere.html.

The Future of "Off-the-Charts," "Unprecedented," and "Record-Breaking"

In the San Francisco Bay Area, the season before Wildfire Season is becoming Heat Wave Season, something we are unprepared for in Northern California where people, including myself, do not have air conditioners—things we haven't needed in summers past. We also don't have basements that could provide a cooler refuge. It is frequently above 110°F (43°C) in my house. Unfortunately, laying the groundwork for Wildfire Season, Heat Wave Season is accompanied by drought, which means that I can't even leave a sprinkler on to run through with my kids.

The earth is in an exponentially increasing warming trend, and that trend is due to human action. Ice core measurements show that over the last ten thousand years, the temperature rose slightly. At the time of the industrial revolution, the amount of carbon dioxide in the atmosphere shot up and continues rising.[14] If the trend continues, we will continue to break heat records all over the world every season to have one worst-drought-ever replaced by the next-worst-drought-ever the following year, and so on.

The report issued in 2021 by the Intergovernmental Panel on Climate Change predicts that the earth will see an average annual temperature increase of between 1°C and 5°C by 2100.[15] The reason for the large span of possibility is that the ultimate outcome is based on human behavior. The good news is that humans have control over what will happen to our climate; the bad news is also that humans have control over what will happen to our climate. The report shows

---

14   NASA, "Carbon Dioxide Concentration," NASA, March 16, 2023, accessed April 17, 2023, https://climate.nasa.gov/vital-signs/carbon-dioxide/.

15   "Climate Change: Widespread, Rapid and Intensifying," *Intergovernmental Panel on Climate Change*, August 7, 2021, https://www.ipcc.ch/2021/08/09/ar6-wg1-20210809-pr/.

that if carbon dioxide emissions are at net-zero by 2050,[16] the earth's temperature increase will be on the lower end of the spectrum; if carbon dioxide emissions continue to rise at a steady rate, the earth's temperature increase will be on the higher end of the spectrum (and will keep going up).

My first thought upon hearing this news is that 1°C to 5°C doesn't sound that bad. That's roughly between 2°F and 10°F, and I often live through temperature changes like that in a single day, not to mention seasonally. But, of course, the prediction refers to an annual global average, and very small changes in annual averages can have huge impacts on the ecosystems and weather patterns worldwide. To give you some idea of what this will really means, 251 million years ago the earth saw the Permian mass extinction event when the earth's temperature rose 10°C (18°F) very quickly—in earth terms—over the course of ten thousand years. That event killed about 95 percent of life on earth.[17] The earth was about 4½°C (8°F) cooler twenty thousand years ago at the peak of our last ice age when Canada and much of the northern United States were covered in ice sheets a mile thick.[18] When the earth is 3°C (5.4°F) warmer, about 30 percent of all living species around the world will have died off.[19]

16   Ibid.

17   Jana Gilwa, "Gradual Warming Prior to the End-Permian Mass Extinction," *Palaeon-tology*, 65(5), https://doi.org/https://doi.org/10.1111/pala.12559.

18   Michone Scott, "What's the Coldest the Earth's Ever Been?" NOAA Climate. gov, February 18, 2021, https://www.climate.gov/news-features/climate-qa/whats-coldest-earths-ever-been.

19   Benji Jones, "5 Signs of How Climate Change Is Unraveling Earth's Ecosystems," Vox, March 1, 2022, https://www.vox.com/down-to-earth/2022/3/1/22954531/climate-change-ipcc-wildlife-extinction.

On our current trajectory, the earth will be 4½°C (8°F) warmer on average annually by 2100.[20] But it isn't just the rise in temperature that we need to consider, it is also the rate at which we are raising the temperature. Past dramatic changes in temperature have happened over the course of tens of thousands of years. Animals and plants have had thousands of years to migrate and evolve in order to survive. Things are moving much more quickly now.

The difference between a 1.5°C (2.7°F) rise in temperature and 2°C (3.6°F) rise is. 06 meters of sea level rise.[21] If you live on an island nation or near the coast, that could be the difference between having a home and not.

Reuters. (2021, November 9). *Tuvalu minister stands in Sea to film COP26 speech to show climate change.* Reuters. https://www.reuters.com/business/cop/tuvalu-minister-stands-sea-film-cop26-speech-show-climate-change-2021-11-08/

20   IPCC, "Global Warming of 1.5°C - Intergovernmental Panel on Climate Change," IPCC, accessed November 15, 2022, https://www.ipcc.ch/sr15/.

21   Andrea Willige, "1.5°C vs 2.0°C: What's in Half a Degree for Climate Change?" Spectra, November 24, 2021, accessed April 17, 2023, https://spectra.mhi.com/1-5-c-vs-2-0-c-whats-in-half-a-degree-for-climate-change.

The foreign minister of the small Pacific island nation of Tuvalu, Simon Kofe, gave a speech to the Climate Summit COP26 in November of 2021, standing in his suit and tie behind a podium knee-deep in water. Sea level rise is slowly flooding his nation. He stated that the current class of pupils "could be the last generation of children to grow up in Tuvalu."

With a 1.5°C raise in temperature we will lose about 70 percent of the world's coral reefs, which is devastating, but with a 2°C rise we will lose more than 99 percent.[23] With a 1.5°C (2.7°F) rse in temperature, 9 percent of the world's population will see extreme heat waves—death, crop failure, etc.—every two decades, with a 2°C (3.6°F) rise, 28 percent of the world's population will experience this.[24] However, these are impacts that don't just abruptly start and end at a single temperature. The more warming we can prevent, the better off our future world will be.

> ## QUOTE OF THE DAY
>
> *"Limiting warming to one and a half degrees Celsius is possible within the laws of chemistry and physics, but doing so would require unprecedented changes."* – **Jim Skea**[22]

Greater warming will mean greater changes that are progressively more difficult to manage. Due to that already-executed credit card debt of carbon dioxide released into the atmosphere, and a slew of other variables, it's possible that this will result in an additional 1°C (1.8° F) of warming in the next thirty years, which adds to the 1°C (1.8°F) increase in temperature we've seen in the past century.[25]

---

22   Jim Skea, Professor of Sustainable Energy at Imperial College London and co-chair of the IPCC Working Group III.

23   Ibid.

24   Ibid.

25   NASA, "Climate Change Evidence: How Do We Know?" NASA, March 2, 2023, https://climate.nasa.gov/evidence/.

We know that in the past, small increases in the average global temperature have caused crop failures due to disease or pests spreading to new areas or drought and that food stress has led to the demise of vibrant civilizations. The fall of major empires all coincided with periods of climate instability: the Mayan civilization (one thousand years ago, droughts),[26] the Roman empire (two thousand years ago, volcanic activity triggered a mild ice age that lasted for 150 years),[27] and ancient Egypt (five thousand years ago, a change in the Nile's flooding patterns due to volcanic activity).[28]

A valid question is: Why isn't every government in the world reacting with everything they have to slow down climate change?

We are capable of major change. During the COVID-19 pandemic, we saw not only governments but also private institutions, businesses, and individuals make sudden and drastic changes. The San Francisco Bay Area came to a grinding halt. California had one of the most conservative responses in the country. The government enacted regulations (no large gatherings, certain public places closed); businesses asked employees to work online from home and began pickup and delivery services; people stayed six feet away from one another. I closed my offices for a solid year and a half. We held weekly meetings and stayed in touch by email and phone

26 Robin D. Wordsworth, et al., "The Climate of Early Mars | Annual Review of Earth and Planetary Sciences," Impacts of Climate Change on the Collapse of Lowland Maya Civilization, May 11, 2016, accessed April 8, 2022, https://www.annualreviews.org/doi/abs/10.1146/annurev-earth-060115-012355.

27 Kyle Harper, "How Climate Change and Plague Helped Bring down the Roman Empire," Smithsonian.com, December 19, 2017, accessed April 19, 2022, https://www.smithsonianmag.com/science-nature/how-climate-change-and-disease-helped-fall-rome-180967591/.

28 Robin D. Wordsworth, et al., "The Climate of Early Mars | Annual Review of Earth and Planetary Sciences," Impacts of Climate Change on the Collapse of Lowland Maya Civilization, May 11, 2016, accessed April 8, 2022. https://www.annualreviews.org/doi/abs/10.1146/annurev-earth-060115-012355.

calls. My life partner stayed glued to his phone, taking work calls on the other side of the house. The schools closed, and my kids were suddenly home daily trying to stay focused on Zoom classes. We were all on video conference calls of some kind, learning how to screenshare and blur our backgrounds so that no one could see our messy houses. I ordered groceries online to be delivered. Local farmers, no longer able to sell fresh food at the farmer's markets, also started delivery services. What we couldn't get locally we got from Amazon.

But the difference between climate change and COVID-19 is scope. Climate change not only has a global scope, like COVID-19, but one that is lasting and diverse. Climate change reveals itself over decades or centuries with a variety of effects that we see (and don't see). Climate change affects more than humans, it encompasses every ecosystem. And it is not caused by not just one industry or a single source, but by many different industries and many different types of impacts. We cannot swab the nose of a problem or take its temperature at the door and definitely say that it is positive for climate change impacts.

Originally published by Rand McNally in 1931.[29]

---

29   Nick Routley, "The Histomap: 4000 years of World History," Visual Capitalist, retrieved from https://www.visualcapitalist.com/histomap/.

What Can We Do?

The effects of climate change are hitting home. Countries are being economically impacted by fires, hurricanes, flooding, and other natural disasters. While governments are responding with incentives and regulations, there is a lot that we can do as individuals, and especially as business leaders and leaders of industries. Business leaders and leaders of industries are the changemakers and can bring to life the types of sweeping innovation and structural changes throughout the industry we are going to need for real impacts. And they can take advantage of business and growth opportunities along the way—there are a lot of ways to do that. I would argue that every leader in every industry can find over one hundred ways to innovate and get a triple win by impacting climate change, becoming more competitive, and making their businesses more profitable through a single effort.

Environmental, Social, and Governance (ESG) criteria was introduced in 2006 through a United Nations report.[30] The idea grew out of business philosophies around sustainability and socially responsible investing. The goal of ESG is to provide a measurement of a company's environmental, social, and governance behaviors for potential investors who can then screen companies based on how they meet these standards to decide how and where they want to invest. It's sort of like looking at reviews of a hotel and seeing that most people were happy with the quality of the bed but a little disappointed in the free breakfast. Embedding ESG factors in capital markets makes good business sense. It leads to more sustainable markets, better outcomes for societies, and profits for business. Investors are responding, allocating trillions of dollars to ESG funds and stocks related to companies

---

30   United Nations, "An Introduction to the Principles for Responsible Investment," accessed August 2023, www.swedfund.se/media/1038/un-pri-principles-for-responsible-investment.pdf.

that support policies and practices around ESG. ESG is an economic wave, and it is here, and it is here to stay.

ESG business statements include environmental goals such as ways to protect the environment by considering their own carbon footprint and the carbon footprints of associated industries, biodiversity, deforestation, and corporate policies to address climate impact. However, it also includes related topics that business hasn't historically considered side by side with environmental goals. Social goals focus on how a company builds and maintains all internal and external relationships (employees, suppliers, customers, communities) including racial justice, pay equity, health and safety, and human capital. Governance goals can be divided by internal governance and external governance. Internal governance has to do with promoting teamwork, individual empowerment and integrity, and communicating within the office (everything from making sure that the human resources handbook is regularly updated to creating a culture that encourages people to interact). External governance pertains to a company's code of ethics, zero tolerance behavior policy, and social responsibility. The goal of ESG is to switch people on morally, especially businesspeople in positions of power (and maybe to make morality a competitive advantage and go for the triple win with that effort).

MEME-WORTHY

The crux of the social aspect, as corny and meme-worthy as it sounds, is that we're all in this together; we share a planet and need to treat people fairly and equally to thrive together.

Stuck in the Middle With You

But this isn't just about feel-good moments; sustainability has many meanings, and businesses that want to survive going forward (to sustain) will need to embrace and excel at establishing and following ESG criteria. At the end of the day, ESG is more than the investing benchmark upon which it was founded, it is now a consumer benchmark. Consumers support businesses that treat employees fairly, contribute to environmental stability, and care about the communities that they serve.

Take Action: Be a Conscious Consumer (A Great Place to Start)

I had the honor of meeting Dr. Jane Goodall, as in world-renowned-expert-on-chimps Jane Goodall. She was a speaker at a Young Presidents' Organization (YPO) event in London, talking to a bunch of CEOs about conservation and telling stories about her research. This was after she'd starred in an ad for an underwear company called Boody.

At the YPO event, someone asked Dr. Goodall about starring in the commercial. She smiled and said of Boody, "They're really an amazing sustainable company." Then she told us the story of the underwear commercial. Representatives from Boody first asked her to appear in the commercial in a pair of their underwear and nothing else, to which she said, "Oh, no. Definitely not." Then they suggested that she could also wear a shirt, to which she said, in a Dr. Goodall way, "That's not going to happen."

The final ad shows men and women of various ethnicities and body types (although mainly young and gorgeous) modeling underwear in a lush jungle. Dr.

HOMEWORK: WATCH THIS

Watch the Boody ad here:

Goodall, fully clothed and also gorgeous and stately, in a long-sleeved sweater and pants, provides the voice-over: "Humans. What unusual animals we are." Then we see Dr. Goodall in the foreground, now in her late eighties, white hair tied back in a casual ponytail, somehow looking both regal and approachable. She is looking up through the jungle to the sky where a rocket aims upward. Her voice-over continues. "Off we search for new worlds with so much to do on the one we leave behind. It's a big job making our world a better place. But getting started, that's as easy as changing your underwear."

I DIDN'T STEAL JANE GOODALL'S PURSE

But out of curiosity, I wanted to. Here's what I imagine was in there:

- A bamboo comb and hair tie
- Not-tested-on-animals lip balm (recycled tree salve, cherry flavor)
- A mobile phone with contacts of all the world leaders
- A small framed picture of the chimps she loved
- Youth elixir given to her by a chimpanzee
- Heaps of antianxiety and high blood pressure management medications necessary after decades of outreach trying to get humans to act on environmental issues

After the conference, I looked up Boody, the company that had gotten Jane Goodall to do an underwear commercial. Boody is the first Australian/New Zealand underwear brand to become a B Corp certified business, meaning that they meet standards of accountability, transparency, and performance, and they are a 1 percent for the planet participant, which means they donate to environmental partners. They manufacture their undies from forest stewardship council certified bamboo, which is environmentally sustainable. And this is what they highlight in their ads. Their marketing strategy, unlike other underwear brands, is not about making the wearer feel sexy, or even comfortable (although their underwear is comfortable), it is about providing an ethical choice to consumers. It appeals to morals. And it works. It ends up that people like to feel good about themselves in deeper ways than sex appeal.

Consumerism is a powerful force. Consumers take into account their own ethical, social, and environmental values before committing to purchasing. Right now, this consciousness is most pronounced in places like Asia and Latin America where consumers have obvious, firsthand experiences of climate change, but we live in a global and informed world, and this is a growing consideration of consumers worldwide. Companies that meet ESG goals now may be doing so to their advantage in terms of gaining and retaining customers, but companies that don't address these crucial issues will be out of business very quickly. Getting on board is "as easy as changing your underwear," according to Boody. Small steps and small decisions, while themselves are not enough, do lead to larger initiatives. Consider alternatives to the way that you do business or who you do business with. Innovate. Change the way you produce existing products. Change your operating model. Reduce your electricity consumption. Reduce your overall impact on the planet and communicate.

In her speech at the YPO event, Dr. Goodall told some stories about working in Africa with chimpanzees. At some point she recognized that the chimpanzee habitats were disappearing, trees slashed and burned as urban areas encroached, or people leveled land for agriculture. Dr. Goodall went into town to try to advocate for the chimpanzees, but no one cared about animals living in the bush, they were worried about their own lives and their own survival. If she wanted to secure a future for the chimpanzees, she needed to do work beyond the boundaries of the jungle where they lived. She needed to take on a bigger role and not only advocate for the chimpanzees that she loved but also for their environment. She left her chimpanzees.

Flying back to London, she looked out the plane window and saw an aerial view of the jungle. She could see the destruction in its entirety. The scale was unbelievable. Until that moment, she really had not been able to see the forest through the trees.

For years after she worked with governments and local environmental organizations, she became an educator in addition to an advocate. She dedicated her life to the conservation of the jungle where the chimpanzees lived. Years later she flew back to the jungle and got the same aerial view, but now the jungle had been restored. Instead of scorched debris, trees were growing. Her efforts had paid off. If one woman can save a jungle, imagine what thousands, or tens of thousands, or millions, or eight billion advocates can do for the planet.

A quote from Dr. Jane Goodall appears at the end of the Boody ad: "You cannot go through a single day without having an impact on the world around you. What you do makes a difference, and you have to decide what kind of difference you want to make."

We are all consumers, and being consumers gives us power. Here are ways that you can yield that power to make an impact on climate change.

Tier 1: The Savvy At-Home Composter

1. Look for labels like "climate pledge friendly" on Amazon or carbon dioxide emissions ratings (like nutritional information on food packaging, many products now carry climate scores, sustainable fishing labeling, etc.)

2. Talk to your family and friends about what you are doing and what you have learned.

31 University of York, Sustainable Seafood Labels, Sustainable Seafood, Future Learn,retrieved from https://www.futurelearn.com/info/courses/ tackling-environmental-challenges/0/steps/151625.

32 Image by Freepik

33 Amazon.com, Climate Pledge Friendly, Making Sustainable Shopping Simpler, retrieved May 10, 2023, from https://sustainability.aboutamazon.com/environment/ sustainable-products.

3. Buy reusable products (cloth napkins, storage containers, etc.).
4. When you can't buy reusable products, buy recyclable products and those made from recyclable goods.
5. Avoid individually packaged items or items that use excess packaging.
6. Avoid fast fashion—go with cool, individual styles.
7. Invest in an electric car.

Tier 2: The CEO Environmental Powerhouse

1. Carefully consider and manage where you spend your company's money. Formal investments as well as team-building events and Christmas parties can be viewed with a sustainable mindset. Your employees will see the intentional and considerate ways that your company spends money and react favorably.
2. Conscious consumerism is powerful, and it is not just for the individual consumer but for the corporate consumer as well. Review your supply chain up and down stream. Understand how your materials are sourced and be clear on where your product or service ends up. It will help you maximize your market share as well as set you up to make more positive corporate consumer decisions.
3. Also take the Tier 1: Savvy At-Home Composter actions.

Tier 3: The Big Cheese World Changer

1. Invest in companies that have an Impact Report that measures and reports the company's carbon footprint and respective actions.
2. Ensure your portfolios have an eye toward climate change. The businesses in which you invest will be impacted by climate change; you need to know their risk mitigation plans or strategies.
3. Also take the Tier 2: CEO Environmental Powerhouse actions.
4. Also take the Tier 1: Savvy At-Home Composter actions.

CHAPTER 2

You Get the Cake and You Get to Eat It Too

The Hippie Gets It from Amazon

I am always conscious of trying to avoid food waste—it makes me crazy because it's so avoidable. Whenever I go to a restaurant, I take reusable collapsible food containers (a Tier 1: Savvy At-Home Composter move). They're superior to the restaurant provided Styrofoam boxes and tinfoil wraps that dump over in your car or leak coconut curry stink that will be with you months later. My containers have snap-on lids that seal; they can go in the microwave or freezer; they look pretty in my fridge; and they fold into flat slabs that fit into my purse.

The waiters are always impressed, as are other customers, which is why I have a spiel about the benefits of reusable containers. I'm a walking ad for these things.

ANGEL'S POSSIBLE ADS FOR REUSABLE CONTAINERS

Don't eat like a Hoover. Pack up your leftovers.

Price of eating out going up? Get your money's worth and bring that excessive American portion size home for another few meals.

Had your fill? Pack the rest. No spill!

Are you tired of single-use takeout containers piling up in landfills? Do you want to make a positive impact on the environment while enjoying your delicious meals?

Look no further! Our reusable containers are designed with convenience and sustainability in mind. No more messy spills in your bag! Our containers feature airtight lids that lock in freshness and prevent leaks, so you can transport your leftovers worry-free.

Going to a steak-out? Be prepared for takeout.

By opting for reusable containers, you're reducing waste and minimizing your carbon footprint. Join the movement toward a greener future!

Reduce waste. Savor taste!

Durable & Safe: Our containers are crafted from high-quality materials, ensuring they withstand repeated use and keep your food secure. They are also BPA-free, guaranteeing the safety of your meals.

Versatile & Stylish: With a variety of sizes and sleek designs, our containers suit every culinary creation. From hearty stews to flavorful salads, your leftovers will look great and taste even better.

Restaurant Discounts: Many partnering restaurants offer exclusive discounts when you bring your reusable container. Enjoy savings while making a positive impact—talk about a win-win!

Join us in embracing sustainability, one meal at a time. Together, we can make a difference and reduce waste in our communities. Let's preserve the planet while relishing every bite!

When I own a restaurant, I'm going to upcharge the meals slightly, and when customers need a doggie bag, I'm going to provide reusable containers with my logo and website printed on the lid. It's a triple win, and I always like to go for at least a triple win (this time a quadruple win):

1. I will be reducing food waste,
2. I will be able to market my environmentally conscious choice,
3. I'll be providing a great product, and
4. (for the bonus) when customers reuse their containers to bring lunch to the office, there's my logo for everyone to see—free advertising.

"Where did you get that?" the waitstaff asks, as do the people I'm eating with and patrons leaning over from other tables

They are probably expecting me to name an obscure co-op, or to tell them a friend brought them home from Sweden.

"On Amazon," I answer, "where you get everything."

RESTAURANTS I WOULD LIKE TO START

Du Taco: a taco truck in Paris

Sandy's: a taco truck at the beach in the San Francisco Bay Area

Clyde's Breakfast and Beer Garden: a farm-to-table restaurant in Oklahoma

There Are No Rules

People often have an all-or-nothing idea when it comes to being environmentally conscious. We can mistakenly think that the only way to be environmentally conscious means only buying products that are produced and sold locally or buying almost nothing at all. Or maybe that to be environmentally conscious we must grow our own fruits and vegetables, mill our own grain, milk our own animals, and weave the fabric for our clothes. Or even more extreme, if we cannot grow it or make it ourselves, we should trade our wares and skills for life's necessities. Many people incorrectly assume that being environmentally conscious means having no indulgences, basically becoming suburban monks.

Screw that. Life is way too short.

I have complete respect for monks and admire the dedication of people who want to live like them, so long as they don't judge others for being environmentally conscious in different ways or accuse me of not being environmentally conscious at all because I like the convenience of two-day delivery and fancy soap from Europe. (In fact, most people whom I encounter indicate they are willing to make lifestyle changes to help prevent climate change, and that is great news.) We need to change the conversation around environmentalism to one that will work for humanity. Humans want stuff. I want to strike this *balance* when it comes to being environmentally conscious.

REMEMBER THE '50S?

The post-war era when magazine advertisements showed robotic gadgets to simplify life alongside DIY bomb shelter kits that could be built in a backyard. People were both accumulating materialistic comforts and also reacting to the fear of nuclear war and major social change. There was an ongoing dynamic between comfort-seeking and threat-averting behaviors. We are here again—another pivotal point in human history when we find ourselves on the very brink of self-annihilation but also wanting Roombas, wall-size flat screen TVs, and apps that create memes of our holiday pictures. Humans can be anxious and excited at once, risk-taking and security-seeking; we can work hard and have a good time.

Actually the word *balance* is usually bullshit. This suggests that life and the world are stable, like a scale with similar measurements. When I say balance, I mean the kind of balance a surfer feels when she catches a wave. Life is a ride. I want to learn to get on, to stay on, to move with the world around me. That doesn't mean equal parts on either side; it means shifting my weight constantly to find ways to have a good time in the world without destroying it.

A LITTLE MORE ABOUT BALANCE

People tend to think of balance as making things equal or even: One pound of joy-seeking behavior balanced by one pound of environmentally conscious sacrifice. But what I mean by balance is not stabilizing yourself, but adjusting constantly to accommodate your needs and desires with the demands and needs of the greater environment and situation. In this way balance becomes more about awareness, which ultimately is all we really need.

There isn't a formula for riding this wave. There are no rules. Nothing is right all the time for everyone, and no wave is like another. Drawing tight boundaries that define what is environmentally conscious and what is not only serves to exclude people and limit life in ways that are lame and boring and thus will not be adopted. It's a little like throwing a party where you don't allow booze, snacks, music, or talking above a whisper. Who wants to attend that party? And who made you the host anyway?

I coined the term "green-gating" after several interactions with friends, colleagues, and complete strangers who judged me and others as not being environmentally conscious enough. Green-gating is the act of immediately counteracting or devolving a positive environmentally conscious statement or action into a negative one. If I say, "I take my reusable containers to the restaurant," the green-gate response is, "but you buy them from a big corporation." If I say, "I own a farm," the green-gate response is, "But you also own a corporation." If I say, "I compost," the green-gate response is, "But you took a plane to

Italy." Green-gating disregards positive behavior and instead focuses on negative actions and inactions; it creates an argument rather than reveling in a result. The first problem with this attitude is that it fails to acknowledge the materialistic part of being human, that part that wants to party and is willing to make sacrifices, but only if there is also reward. The larger problem is that green-gating does exactly what we don't want engagements around environmentalism to do: It alienates people who could be a part of the conversation and bigger-picture solutions.

In addition to green-gating people's individual lifestyle choices, we also green-gate whole sectors. We love to hate corporations for example. Green-gating a corporation often means dismissing any environmental actions they take as tricks and lies to make money. Of course, sometimes it is tricks and lies. Can corporations have negative impacts? Sure. Do corporations sometimes represent themselves falsely to make a profit?

BAY-AREA BATSHIT

(As in batshit crazy) is another term I coined (I'm inventing words all over the place) to refer to the specific green-gating I often find in my neck of the woods. In the Bay Area, I often encounter very smart people who take extreme and alienating positions around environmentalism.

Absolutely. Are all corporations evil empires? Definitely not. While casting corporations as "bad" simplifies things and makes for easy-to-follow plots in action movies, if we disregard corporations as "evil" or any person as "not environmentally conscious enough," we play an us-and-them game and miss an opportunity to support and encourage change.

Climate activists who come out swinging with heavy-handed warnings and holier-than-thou recommendations (that often slant

49

research or overstate outcomes) risk working against the very action they are trying to promote. "My way or the highway" rules just don't work; people rebel against them because they aren't, well, sustainable. These judgments and demands create the dynamic of an angry parent yelling at a teenager about appropriate attire. Does it really matter if the cap has gory graphics from your kid's favorite band? In a crisis, we really just need it to protect them from the sun. We need to let go of rules for the sake of rules and focus on what's important.

I get this type of exclusionary judgment from both sides. I get judged for being too hippie and carrying my hippie bag of tricks everywhere, and I also get judged for not packing enough into my hippie bag of tricks. Both sides are telling me that I don't fit in. In a way both sides are telling me, "No," which as an entrepreneur is a familiar line and one that I take as a challenge. What do you mean I can't be both? Watch this.

Forget the rules. Forget finding an eternally stable balance. Catch the wave and ride.

Bank Loan of Global Resources

I have avid allergies. I am constantly sneezing and blowing my nose. It's not awesome. Also not awesome was the amount of tissue I was going through—box after box. It felt really wasteful. When I noticed the pile of tissues in the garbage, I also noticed that I was doing the same with paper towels in the kitchen. I decided to switch to cloth that I can wash and reuse. Check out my triple win: 1) It looks nice, 2) it's gentler to my nose and hands, 3) it doesn't overflow the garbage, and for the bonus, and 4) now I feel better about my actions. I realized that I can make that type of transition easily, and compounded with other actions, this can make a tangible impact on the environment.

I started thinking about other things that I could do that would cost me relatively little effort, make my life better, and be environmentally conscious. A friend suggested dryer balls. Simple. They help the dryer work more efficiently, clothes dry faster, and I'm paying less of an electric bill.

In this way, I added to my environmentally conscious actions little by little by observing my day-to-day life, thinking about my impact on the environment, and making small changes. As bigger choices came into my life, I was already in the habit of thinking this way. When I decided to move to a more remote location (because I hate people), I knew I would be driving more, so I bought an electric car.

SPREADSHEETS THAT SHOULD NEVER EXIST

- Snack Choices
- Alcohol Consumption
- "Sad Hour"
- Sexual Partners
- Sci-Fi Movies Watched

I talked to my MIT scholar friend who had been calculating his own carbon footprint for twenty-five years (another Tier 1: Savvy At-Home Composter move). He has a spreadsheet where he calculates his daily activities. It was inspiring. I thought, "I can do that," and then I did what any normal person does, and I Googled to learn more. It ends up there are tons of resources to help you calculate your carbon footprint by answering simple questions. You don't need to know what activities emit greenhouse gas to use these, they walk you through it. I tend to rely on my intuition, rather than my math skills, when estimating these, assuming that throwing away a tissue is not the same carbon assault as having a steak dinner.

A NOTE ABOUT RESOURCES

The editor and publisher would love me to list sources for you here, but it is my firm belief that figuring this out for yourself is your first step to taking action. Besides, it's like an internet scavenger hunt. It will be fun. And this stuff is super easy to find, and if you are interested, you will take the initiative and find it on your own. Here are some search terms to start with: "Carbon Calculator" and "Calculate Carbon Footprint."

For once, Dr. Tatiana and I agree.

But as a human, I'm not always able, or willing, to eliminate my carbon footprint. I'm an executive, and I fly a lot. At one time I had seven or eight offices around the country from which I worked in addition to attending conferences and meetings around the world and taking trips—because I like to go places. I knew this wasn't good in terms of my carbon footprint. I did some research (Google again) and learned that planes expend the most fuel during takeoff and landing. Since then I have cut my fuel usage by only taking direct flights, but I'm not willing to give up flying altogether. Until they invent solar-powered 747s, I will be putting carbon into the atmosphere.

People of all socioeconomic levels have desires for growth that are costly to the environment. Wealthy people living in the Bay Area want seven flat-screen TVs, to fly around in their private jets, and other things they consider luxuries. We can't combat the human desire to progress socioeconomically and materialistically. My idea is not to fight these

A NOTE FROM DR. TATIANA

As we refine our understanding of our impacts, the best sources for this information will change over time.

human desires, but to understand the impacts and work with that understanding to still solve the problem.

I realized that I couldn't get to net-zero carbon dioxide emissions by eliminating my carbon use (both because of my lifestyle choices and the world I live in). I needed a new way to think about my interaction with the environment. Now that I was tracking my own carbon footprint and could see the carbon I was putting into the atmosphere, I developed a Tier 1 personal recovery plan.

WHY PERSONAL CHANGE MATTERS

As Dr. Tatiana continually points out to me, real change will not be brought about by personal actions, but by changes made by entire industries and governments. However, industries and governments are made of people. Personal change, while it makes a small impact, is important as a way of helping individuals understand how human actions cause climate change as well as the ways that these actions can be eliminated are counteracted and increasing awareness and engagement of individual people who in turn put pressure on governments and industries. The risk of focusing on personal change is that we lose sight of the larger (and more significant) project of transforming the large institutions that can make the necessary impacts for real change.

I think of working toward net-zero carbon dioxide emissions like a bank loan that uses global resources rather than money. If I take out a loan from the earth in terms of global resources, I need to pay back that loan with interest in order to achieve a net negative. Air travel creates a carbon footprint. I wanted to go to Italy. I went to Italy, and when I came home, I planted some trees and put carbon back into the earth. It wasn't hard, I got to feel good about myself for being environmentally conscious, and I got to enjoy some great pasta. On a grander scale, in order to continuously pay back my constant debt from frequent travel, I own a farm that offsets the carbon expenditure of my companies and personal use through the carbon sequestration of regenerative farming.

So have your car, go on vacation, take out your loan. And pay it back with interest. As with money in a bank, the earth's resources are not infinite; as with taking out a loan from a bank, there are consequences, but those consequences are manageable. You can take out a big loan so long as you are willing to pay back a greater amount. We have to pay back our loans. Aside from that, we can do whatever we want. I am determined to have my cake and eat it too. We have far more options for combining survival and opulence than ever before. You don't have to live like a hippie to work for a better world. You need to learn some stuff, take initiative, set goals, and ride the wave.

A WAKE-UP CALL FROM DR. TATIANA

Planting trees is not equivalent to paying back the debt of burning fossil fuels. Fossil fuels were previously in deep storage; they were not exchanging carbon with the atmosphere. Trees are part of a living system, which exchanges carbon with the atmosphere regularly through things like photosynthesis, respiration, growth, and decomposition.

Trees that we plant now pay back the debt of deforestation done by previous generations. Planting trees also makes progress on humanity's other debts to nature and slows or offsets the impacts of burning fossil fuels, but there is no way to truly pay back the debt of burning fossil fuels.

The Gulch Environmental Foundation

I was so annoyed by following other people's stupid rules that I started my own foundation and made my own rules.

My organizations have always been philanthropic, but as I began to seriously look at getting myself, working on Tier 2 goals for the CEO Environmental Powerhouse, and getting my businesses to net-zero, I began to more closely scrutinize what was happening to the hundreds of thousands of dollars that I was donating to environmental efforts. It seemed like the money went into a black hole of death. I didn't know what it was being used for or how it was making a difference.

I started trying to be involved by volunteering to do physical labor for the actions to which I was donating money so that I could better understand what these organizations were up to. I took some of my employees to help with fire restoration, river cleanup, bike building, etc. We'd show up ready for a day of hard work, and the same thing would always happen: Just as we were getting on a roll, we'd run out of work. It ends up most corporations attend these work sessions for the photo op, not because they're expecting to get anything done.

I LOVE ME A LITTLE JOKE

In the past decade, I spent about $200,000 donating to environmental charities in Donald Trump's name. It's a win for everyone: 1) I get a good laugh, 2) environmental charities get funding, and 3) Donald Trump (unwittingly) is part of doing something good for the environment.

My breaking point was when I showed up with my Motive Power team to plant trees by a freeway to help improve the air quality around the urban school located there. We arrived to find equipment and trees ready for us ("staged" would be a better word), and we began to plant. We had all the trees planted in an hour. The project manager congratulated us and offered to snap a picture that I could post on my website.

"We came out here to work," I said to the manager. "We want to plant more trees."

"That was your allotment," the manager told me.

"What about all those trees over there?" I asked, pointing to more staging.

"Those are Bank of America's trees," the project manager told me. Bank of America was coming for their photo op the next week.

I SHOULD MENTION

(Both out of pride and because, while I'm willing to work hard, I also like to have fun) I snuck a keg (not a six pack) of beer onto the field where we were planting...which was on school grounds...during school hours... and didn't get caught...even when the principal came out to thank us for planting trees.

"They're our trees now," I said, and my team and I stole the Bank of America's trees (sorry, Bank of America, it was nothing personal). After we planted those, we moved on to steal the next lot and so on until all the trees were planted.

The environmental agencies to which I was donating also seemed focused on appearance. I couldn't see the impact they were having. I was frustrated, but I'm an entrepreneur, so I stepped up to the Tier 3: Big Cheese World Changer level and created my own organization. With the Gulch Environmental Foundation, I can track and report my investment the way I would for a business. Not only can a donor see where her money is going when she contributes to the Gulch Environmental Foundation, but any contribution can be tracked, dollar for dollar, to the direct impact it has on the environment.

MANY CEOS HAVE THEIR OWN PHILANTHROPIC ORGANIZATIONS

...so that they can have control of where their funds go in exactly this way. Here are some I like:

- Bain & Company (https://www.bain.com/about/further/social-impact/)
- Bill and Melinda Gates Foundations (https://www.gatesfoundation.org)
- Ron Finley Project (https://ronfinley.com)
- Patagonia (https://www.patagonia.com/how-we-fund/)

And my own, of course:

- The Gulch Environmental Foundation (https://gulchfoundation.org)

The Gulch Environmental Foundation has two founding principles. One is that donations never go to administrative or salary expenses—the organization's purpose is making a real impact on the environment. The second is that project reporting is available to investors explaining not only where their money went but also the initial impact and the progression of that impact on the environment. If you donate $10 to the Gulch Environmental Foundation, you can see that your $10 was used to plant this tree and that the tree has been in the ground for three years.

The first projects that the Gulch Environmental Foundation attempted had to do with fire reclamation. Northern California had been ravaged by wildfires, and some of my friends' houses had burned down. I learned from their experiences the difficulties of cleaning up after a fire. It's a hazmat situation. You can't just rebuild, you need to excavate, run chemical tests, replenish the area, then deal with insurance companies and other agencies. It is expensive and invasive.

Starting a regenerative farm was another project. The project that I would name Rainmaker Farm had some direct objectives aimed at combating carbon dioxide emissions. The first was to increase the carbon held in soils on agricultural land (we would prove that we had done this collaborating with the local university to analyze soil samples), and the second was to demonstrate the transition from conventional to regenerative/no-till farming—a practice that improves carbon capture. Rainmaker Farm also required employees from all of my organizations and invited other people (friends, family, school groups, other organizations) to literally put their hands in the dirt and have a physical impact on combating climate change (no limited allotment of trees or focus on photo ops). Like all the projects supported by the Gulch Environmental Foundation, Rainmaker Farm produces observable impacts. We named the farm "Rainmaker" not after strip clubs nor because of the copious amounts of money it cost or generated, but because changing the way land is managed can change the local microclimates and, on very large scales, change the patterns of rain.

A NOTE FROM DR. TATIANA

There are ranking systems for nonprofits so you can make sure you are giving to impactful organizations* such as Charity Watch, Giving Compass, and Charity Navigator. These rate charities on a variety of metrics, including impact and financial accountability.

*Dr. Tatiana wanted to give you the web addresses for these systems, but again, I am confident in your ability to use Google.

Take Action: Consider Your Debt

Right now the conversation around being environmentally conscious is a "No" conversation. "No, you are not doing enough." "No, you could never do that." "No, that will never work." It ends up, this is great for me. It makes me look harder to find solutions.

I was once on a panel with another consultant discussing green energy. The consultant didn't like me, probably because I drank too much, and we were competitors, which meant she had to out-consultant me. She argued that solar energy was only for rich people and not a viable option for the general public. Her arguments sided with the utilities, who were her potential clients, and expressed the barriers utilities faced to adopting green energy.

She used the line, "rich people in California," as in, "only rich people in California can afford solar," because she knew that I was rich and from California, and she also knew what her East Coast clients from the coal states thought of Californians.

Her statement, of course, sent me on a spiteful hunt for information that I could use to refute her the next time we were on a panel together. I learned from a wholesale solar company not only how solar systems are created but also that an entire system with a battery backup for an average-size family home can be purchased and installed for around $10,000 total. While $10,000 is a lot, it isn't out of range—it's less than the cost of a car, the payment plans are better, and it pays itself off over time. Solar is accessible, even for low-income families.

Because a determined woman on a panel told me, "No, it could not be done," I learned all about the possibilities, which says more about me than it does about solar panels. As I said in the introduction, I often do my best work out of spite.

And there are solutions, tons of them, but we have to first think differently about being environmentally conscious and getting to net-zero. This is not an either/or scenario. If we make it about deprivation and suffering, people (including me) will never do it. We need to find a way to have our cake and eat it too—because who just wants to sit at the table and stare at a piece of cake? This has to do with understanding the impacts of our resource use (knowing our debt) and finding ways to reduce and/or offset this debt with measures that will aid in slowing climate change. Here are some ways that you can understand your impact on climate change and take action to reduce or offset that impact.

Tier 1: The Savvy At-Home Composter

1. Calculate how much carbon dioxide you put into the atmosphere by using one of the many online carbon-footprint calculators.
2. Choose actions that fit your life:
   - Look for ways to reduce your use of fossil fuels.
   - Look up ways to put carbon back into the earth—mostly—growing things in your yard, community gardens, or other areas.
   - Pick up trash when you see it.
   - Look for sustainable energy options in your area, there may now be more options than you realize.
   - Be aware of your personal impact to help you balance your actions and drive conversations in your family.
3. Vote and be active in all levels of government.
   - Remember, although individual lifestyle choices do make a difference collectively, they aren't really what is driving most emissions, and the most impactful thing you can do is support policies that are climate friendly.
4. Talk to your family and friends about what you are doing and what you have learned.

Tier 2: The CEO Environmental Powerhouse

1. Calculate the carbon footprint of your companies so that you know when and how much carbon dioxide your company puts directly and indirectly into the atmosphere.

2. Educate your teams on things like climate impact, where your energy comes from, where your food comes from, greenhouse gases, carbon footprint, etc.

3. Also take the Tier 1: Savvy At-Home Composter actions.

Tier 3: The Big Cheese World Changer

1. High net-worth individuals often migrate to a place of philanthropy after they have secured their wealth. Consider ESG-related philanthropy and/or create such an organization yourself in an area of your choice (something ESG-related that speaks to your passion—be it social or political issues, environmental or national governance in nature). There is a cause waiting for your money. And of course there are the tax write-offs.

> **A NOTE FROM DR. TATIANA**
>
> Make sure that you are using a carbon footprint calculator that takes into account where you live.

2. Prepare your organization for carbon-offset programs that adhere to effective incentives and associated business practices or initiate them yourself. Ultimately this will result in tax savings and feel-good opportunities. If you are Google, why not replant the Amazon rainforest? Soon enough there could be huge tax credits for you as a result, and even if the Amazon replanting is not specific to your industry, if you have the capacity, it could heavily offset your carbon footprint.

3. Require your state, local, and federal governments, congressmen/women, and lobbyists to have relatable knowledge on climate issues to your industry. This will enable better fortification for the conversations needed with policy makers, regulators, and the like.

4. Also take the Tier 2: CEO Environmental Powerhouse actions.

5. Also take the Tier 1: Savvy At-Home Composter actions.

CHAPTER 3

Separation Anxiety: Hollywood and the Heartland

The Heartland

I was now calculating my carbon footprint (Tier 1), and I wanted to offset my lifestyle. One of the best ways to put carbon back into the earth is to grow things, so I decided to buy a farm (Tier 3 since I would be buying and running the farm through the Gulch Environmental Foundation). How hard could farming be? It's like gardening on a grand scale, and I've got gardening figured out. I had a vision: Revolutionize the farming industry by transforming a conventional tilled farm into a regenerative farm . I was going to demonstrate that the farming industry could be symbiotic with the carbon cycle rather than destructive to it. It was an idea about how to make things better, and the entrepreneur in me jumped into action. I began my search for a farm.

BUY THE FARM

To die, to bite the dust, to be called home, to meet your maker, breathe your last breath, perish, meet your demise, slip away, join your ancestors, go to a better place, go west, cross the River Styx, succumb, ultimate end, give up the ghost, take a dirt nap, become worm food, belly-up, toes-up, kaput, go six feet under, push up daisies, join the choir eternal, cash in your chips, kick the bucket, take a final bow, end your earthly career, or maybe rot in hell.

I was doing none of these. But I did buy a farm to participate in this cycle of life. "Worm food" and "pushing up daisies" were very on point.

As someone who owns several financially successful corporations, even I can't afford farmland in the San Francisco Bay Area, where I live, or farmland anywhere in California (that's not on a cliff or a former burn zone) for that matter, so I had to look beyond my own backyard. It wasn't the end of the world—far from it. I love leaving the Bay Area.

Like many places, the Bay Area has become an island unto itself where people with the same political vantage point and social philosophy engage in comfortable conversations that only serve to reinforce their own views. We are like sports fans from one team agreeing that a bad ref cost us the game. The Bay Area isn't unique in this regard. Many communities have similar monocultures that indulge one perspective and label all others as "stupid," "naïve," "uneducated," "impractical," the product of people who "just don't get it," "aren't paying attention," "don't care," or are "brainwashed." It supports a belief system that says, "Anyone who doesn't think like me is a sucker not worth my time."

I have found that monocultures are pervasive not only in my hometown but also in online forums, chosen news sources, and social communities. It's easy to hear your decided-upon beliefs echoed back to you as catchy one-liners, memes, and academic lingo that gives them credence than to confront another opinion. It's human nature to seek this out. Who doesn't like to hear that they're right? The problem with monocultures, of course, is that they are mono-focused and therefore observe only a part of a situation. They have tunnel vision in a landscape where the point is appreciating the horizon. Although the ideals of these monoculture communities are vastly different, they have in common that they are all toxic to communication and unified problem-solving. I'm well aware that in the Bay Area, like in so many places, most people think the same way, and it's easy to get comfortable wallowing in self-righteousness. I don't disagree with everything they espouse, but I do appreciate a broader view. And I like a challenge.

I didn't exactly just throw a dart at a Zillow map of fertile US farmland for sale, I had some specific criteria. I narrowed my search to states that sell land in large parcels for ranching, hunting, and farming: Colorado, Oklahoma, Nebraska, and Kansas. Colorado is closest to California but more arid and with higher elevation. Farming there would be difficult. That brought me to the Heartland. Having grown up and lived my life on the West Coast, most of what I knew about the Heartland I learned from movies and sitcoms featuring jolly, naively friendly, often toothless country folk in suspenders and bonnets standing in front of flat fields full of corn. Ends up Hollywood got some of the costuming right but much of the rest of it wrong.

HERE'S ANOTHER WAY SITCOMS GOT IT WRONG

The opening song of The Beverly Hillbillies labels Jed Clampett a "poor mountaineer" who discovers oil in his backyard. Oil deposits are not discovered near mountains. Sorry, Jed.

I refined my search. I wanted as much land as I could possibly afford (most farms are purchased in cash) that was fertile and farmable. But location also mattered—it needed to be accessible (near a major highway and no more than an hour from a major airport). Not only did I want to go to my farm but I also wanted to bring people there (to educate a broader audience), and that meant getting there needed to be quick and easy.

All of this is fairly easy to research. Google maps will calculate distance and time from airports, and there are other websites that give a full breakdown of the soil content and water reports of farms for sale. I eventually found a 160-acre working farm roughly eighty miles from the Oklahoma City airport for around $300,000.

WHAT ACCESSIBLE MEANS TO ME

Something I've learned as a real-estate owner and head of a corporation is that if you have a second home or location more than an hour from your house, you will never go there. Another attribute of human nature is that we tend toward convenience.

While some of my Hollywood-knowledge of the Heartland proved to be true, many things were nothing at all like I imagined. My 160 acres is not a flat nothingness. It has game in the sense of aesthetic topography; I mean, it's beautiful. There are hills, trees, a creek, and two ponds. Coming from California, 160 acres seemed like a small country. It ended up, as farms go, that it wasn't that big. One hundred and sixty acres is what they refer to in the farm real-estate business as a quarter-section. Mineral rights often determine the way farmland is sold and acquired, which means that unlike that picturesque opening aerial shot in Hollywood movies of neat square fields organized like a patchwork quilt, farmland looks more like, well, an oil splatter. Farmers may own a bit of land in one place and a bit of land in another.

A NOTE FROM DR. TATIANA

The ownership might be scattershot, but the landscape scale patterns are based on 1-mile x 1-mile sections.

I was learning that oil is a big part of the farming industry in Oklahoma. I knew nothing about oil except the little light that comes on in cars every three thousand miles reminding the driver to bring a car in for a change, but it ended up that my 160 acres were right in the middle of an oil field. I knew this for certain because there, on my property, were oil tanks leftover from the last time the land was drilled—something that had not appeared in the photo album online.

We drill oil in California as well, but in Northern California, the oil tanks are politely concealed behind murals painted to look like the natural landscape, and the refineries are far away. In Oklahoma everything is out in the open. This likely speaks a great deal to some of the differences between the Bay Area and Oklahoma.

A NOTE FROM DR. TATIANA

This is largely determined by area. The Richmond Refinery is near the freeway and regularly contaminates the air of nearby residents in the few remaining affordable areas within the San Francisco Bay Area.

For the most part, oil can be extracted without disturbing the farms—aside from being an eye sore. While the oil companies are mostly courteous, in the end they have rights to drill anywhere on the property at any time and to leave their equipment in place (which they often do for years, even after it is no longer in use). Removing the oil tanks from my property was on my to-do list, but first I needed to learn some basics about farming in Oklahoma.

A Fish Out of Water

I expected that starting a farm would mean learning a great deal, but I thought that learning would be focused on crop growth and land management. Instead, I got a cultural education alongside a farming education.

One of the first things I learned was how to get around and understand basic geographic directions. In the Bay Area, people are always moving toward, away from, or alongside the sea or mountains. When you give and get direction, you tell people to go down a particular street toward the ocean, hang a right at the bagel shop on the corner, and park in front of the blue building. In Oklahoma, there are no obviously visible landmarks: no sea, no mountains, no bagel shops. Instead, Oklahomans talk map coordinates and the four cardinal directions. It's an entirely different way of orienting yourself that relies on senses rather than memory. Mastering it requires rewiring your brain to be aware of yourself on a grand scale rather than turn by turn. And mastering this type of orientation is a life-and-death situation in Oklahoma because in the country, people drive big trucks at seemingly ninety miles per hour and yield to traffic moving in a north-south direction—a rule that is known and not indicated by any signage. You better know which way

YOU MIGHT NOT START YOUR OWN FARM

Or you might, but regardless, your path to becoming more environmentally conscious will likely lead you down some new (muddy) paths. Expect to be a fish out of water.

you are headed before you enter an intersection. If I had come to Oklahoma with any lofty ideas about a well-read, well-educated philosophical thinker, I was quickly put in place by anyone who could consistently point to due north.

It wasn't just that I couldn't tell directions, but it was also that I didn't understand the basic laws of physics and nature that any six-year-old having grown up in Oklahoma would have known. When touring the property with the real estate agents, I spotted an enormous tractor tire that had been left on the property. Casually I suggested that I could get a few people to help me move it. The real estate agents and the farmers themselves (another thing I learned is that most farmers need a side-hustle in order to survive) laughed. If you're city-folk like me, you've possibly only encountered a tractor tire as recon-

A NOTE FROM DR. TATIANA

This is specifically an intuitive sense of the cardinal directions.

69

stituted playground equipment. Those are big, but this was a huge solid tire the diameter of a full-grown person that I later learned weighed upward of 600 pounds. Moving one isn't like moving an old couch off your porch, wherein you can offer the neighbors a six-pack for giving you a hand. You need to hire a crane. But I was a CEO with a vision. I was walking around the property and talking possibilities. The real estate agents gave me the sort of smile you give a child who's told you she is going to grow up to be a mermaid, a smile that both affectionately and patronizingly says, "Sure, sweetheart." They had gotten to know me a bit, liked me, and regarded my ignorance as cute.

HERE'S SOMETHING ELSE HEAVY THAT I COULDN'T MOVE

A horse in one instance and a bull in another. Horses weigh in the vicinity of one thousand pounds; bulls can weigh two thousand pounds. They aren't moving unless they are willing to move themselves, but those are stories I will tell later in the book.

But the most eye-opening things that I learned were about the farming industry itself. These I learned as I started to farm and from listening to the stories of other farmers in the community. When I bought the property, the land was being leased to a neighboring farmer who everyone called Farmer Phil. Leasing farmland is common, and Farmer Phil, like most farmers in Oklahoma, both owned his own land and also farmed leased land. Farmer Phil was a seventh-generation farmer, and like everyone in Oklahoma, Phil was inexplicably friendly. Because he was now my tenant, I met him as soon as I purchased the land. He was currently growing wheat, and the crop was not due for harvest for a few months, meaning that Farmer Phil and I would be working together for at least that amount of time.

If a Hollywood director needed to cast an Oklahoma farmer, Farmer Phil would be the guy. He looks and sounds exactly like what you imagine. He's in his midsixties and always dressed in dusty, worn jeans held up by sweet leather suspenders. He wears a baseball cap that shades his bronzed face. In short, he looks like he works hard every day and has worked hard for decades. At our first meeting, he pulled up in his Chevy truck that was caked in mud at the bottom and coated in dust at the top, nearly covering the truck's original gray finish. He had a thick drawl that, in the way of that Yosemite Sam cartoon, emphasized his practiced greetings. Although he did not actually say, "Howdy, y'all," that is pretty much what I heard.

"DARN TOOTIN'"

...is only said by Hollywood actors trying to represent farmers. In my experience, no actual farmer says this. Also "Yee-haw" is not a real thing.

Later I thought that Farmer Phil likely had a similar impression of me: the stereotypical hippie from California. Here was a woman wearing no makeup, without her hair done up (not business professional), having driven to a farm with a dirt road that was not passable in the rain in a little rental car that couldn't have traversed a puddle. My guess is that we were both in many ways exactly what the other was expecting.

It was the start of the COVID pandemic. I was wearing not one but two masks and had been washing my hands incessantly. Farmer Phil wasn't wearing a mask at all, and his hands somewhat matched his truck. We met on my property by the oil tanks.

My first meeting with Farmer Phil was a business meeting, and from my perspective, it did not go well. We needed to negotiate our new relationship. There were different options: I could continue to rent him the land and allow him to farm however he wanted, I could employ him to farm the land the way I wanted, or we could arrange a sort of hybrid situation. I was hoping that Farmer Phil would stay on in some capacity so that I could observe and learn from him, but Farmer Phil was moving away from market crop farming and toward raising cattle. Also, he wanted to retire. That part of our conversation, although bumpy, proved to be the easiest.

"What are you going to do when you retire?" I asked.

"What am I going to do?" he asked. "I'm not going to work," he said, as though perhaps I had never heard of and did not understand the word *retire*.

"I mean, are you going to work on your hobbies, travel, maybe go to a beach?"

"I don't need to go to no beach," Farmer Phil told me. And I thought I had this guy pegged. He didn't know the world. He hadn't traveled. He hadn't thought of anything beyond these acres in Oklahoma. But then Farmer Phil said something that surprised me. "I went to the beach once. Actually I went out to San Francisco. I don't ever need to go back."

He said this very definitely, a proclamation: He'd tried the beach, and he'd tried San Francisco. He'd conducted research, and run an experiment, and San Francisco wasn't his cup of tea.

I nodded.

It was cold outside, and Farmer Phil invited me into his truck where it was warmer. I hesitated. This was still early in the pandemic, and at least in California, COVID restrictions were still in full effect. Getting into a closed vehicle with someone who could have been exposed to COVID and was not masked was exactly what the CDC was warning against at the time. But I opted for social niceties and my desire to get along with this guy.

Farmer Phil and I sat in the cab of his truck, which was indeed warmer, and I watched his breath puff into the still-cool air as he spoke.

It was obvious that he was curious about who I was and why I wanted to own a farm in Oklahoma. He started a careful line of questioning, politely but intelligently questioning me about who I was, why I was there, and what I intended. I was beginning to understand that Farmer Phil was a sort of Columbo, a sharp investigator, his thick drawl and farm-worn jeans strategically putting me at ease while he pursued a thoughtful line of questioning.

DUST BOWL II

"I Think We're to the Dust Bowl." Oklahoma Farmers Say Wheat Crop Is Worst in Decades. -Headline of an article in The Oklahoman, May 2023. [34]

"What do you want to do with this property?" Farmer Phil asked.

"I'm interested in regenerative farming," I told him.

"Regenerative farming, huh? What does that mean to you?"

I introduced my idea of the Rainmaker Farm Project that would transform a conventionally tilled farm into a regenerative no-till farm. I then delved into both the science and philosophy behind such a transformation: reintroducing multiculture farming including livestock incorporation that could increase microbial health and reduce the release of carbon, also resulting in healthier soil that would mean better growth, and diverse plants that would mean more profit and the potential to create microclimates, which would mean more rain and thus even more growth enacting, etc. I was at least teaching and at most preaching, naively seeing myself as an enlightened outsider come to bless the Heartland with my education and ideas. I was making a mistake that often prevents progress in climate change initiatives: I was making assumptions rather than

34   Jordan Green, "'I Think We're to the Dust Bowl.' Oklahoma Farmers Say Wheat Crop Is Worst in Decades," The Oklahoman, May 7, 2023, https://www.oklahoman.com/story/news/2023/05/07/wheat-production-oklahoma-agriculture-farmers-drought-high-winds-declmated-crop/70150182007/.

trying to understand the situation. Regardless of what tier you are on, from the Savvy At-Home Composter to the Big Cheese World Changer, communicating with other people will be necessary to truly make an impact. This means both explaining your ideas and listening to other perspectives. Going into a situation demanding that people see things your way without making an effort to see things their way likely dooms your relationship, and any related progress, to failure. I know this. I am usually far better at communicating, but in that moment, I got carried away and forgot to leave room for Farmer Phil in the conversation. I was not communicating well, but Farmer Phil was very patient.

Farmer Phil easily kept pace with my scientific talk about microbes and process. He took it to the next level and talked about soil contents, runoff patterns, and his observations of different animals migrating across and existing with the land and what those observations told him about the health of his farm and mine. He was educated and also had salt-of-the-earth smarts. He was also deeply reflective, probing consciously into my theories and philosophies. However, like most farmers, Farmer Phil was also pragmatic. "But what's your crop?" Farmer Phil asked.

It ended up that there were a number of things influencing the farming industry in Oklahoma of which I was completely ignorant. One was that there

NAMING THE STRAINS

Another thing I think we can all agree on is the awesome names of marijuana strains. You don't have to partake to appreciate these titles:

- Purple Kush
- Sour Diesel
- Fruity Pebbles
- Pineapple Express
- LA Confidential
- Northern Lights
- Super Silver Haze

was a movement reversing the dust bowl migration of farmers who had left Oklahoma for California; people were coming from California to Oklahoma to farm. There were also international companies, many from China, buying land. All these people, like me, had discovered that they could get good fertile land for cheap in the Heartland. Most of them were coming to grow the profitable and newly legalized crop cannabis.

Oklahoma is on the edge of the Bible Belt. Most of the residents are God-fearing, staunchly religious, and traditional, like Farmer Phil seemed to be. But it ends up that one thing that conservatives and liberals can agree on is the merits of marijuana. In an upset, the people of Oklahoma voted to legalize medical marijuana, and because the opposition had been so certain the bill would not pass, they had not fought for any restrictions. Now pot farms were popping up all over the place, and to Farmer Phil, I seemed a likely candidate for such an endeavor.

I remained oblivious to the issue Farmer Phil was skirting around with his line of questioning that politely indulged my lectures about the merits of multicultural farming and rotating crops that would work symbiotically to replenish the land. He refocused to the issue at hand.

THE PROBLEM WITH POT

I would be supportive of cannabis farming if it were at least regenerative, but like the wine industry in California, it is highly destructive to the soil and land. Some problems with growing cannabis:

- It requires a lot of water.
- Unpermitted growers are destroying wildlife areas.
- The facilities that cultivate cannabis often have high CO2 emissions.[35]

---

35 Jodie Helmer, "The Environmental Downside of Cannabis Cultivation," JSTOR Daily, June 18, 2019, https://daily.jstor.org/the-environmental-downside-of-cannabis-cultivation/.

"But what's your crop?" Farmer Phil persisted.

I named a few that I planned to grow in my rotation: cover crops, wheat, barley, rye, oat, and fruit and nut orchards. Also there would be chickens, cows, maybe goats, and horses?

It seemed we were finally getting to the point, and Farmer Phil was critical. "Why would you want to plant those?" he asked. Farmers like Farmer Phil have needed to move into government-subsidized crops like corn and wheat in order to make a living and sustain their farms. No one is planting cover crops. "Do you have any idea how much seed costs? Don't you know how much it costs to plant ground crops? How do you plan to make money?" He had taken on a tone of both judgment and concern, not knowing what to make of me and also afraid for me. He sounded both like a banker unwilling to give me a loan and a father worried about my life path.

At this point, I made a fatal mistake that entirely turned our conversation.

"I don't need to make money," I told him.

As I watched his eyes react to my words, I attempted to soften the blow. "Not at first."

It was as though I had reached across the truck and slapped his unmasked face. His expression changed; his posture stiffened. It was immediately obvious that I had offended him. Farmer Phil farmed in order to make money or, more to the point, in order to survive and support his family. Every decision was made to that end. He didn't have the luxury of wiggle room here and there or indulging a process that would have increased costs and risk. I hadn't read my audience.

Our conversation was over.

But first Farmer Phil had one more question. He was now done being polite and asked it outright. "Are you planning to grow pot?"

The idea had never occurred to me. "No," I said. "Do people do that?"

"All right then," he said dismissively, moving to start the engine of his truck before I even reached for the door.

I stepped out of the truck, still processing the odd interrogation and the way that his temperament had so quickly shifted. Then he said something that people in Oklahoma always say, and mean, even when you have insulted the way of life they've known for seven generations.

"Let me know if you need help," and he drove away.

Yes, and ...

I did need help later, and I had an excuse to try again with Farmer Phil. First, I needed a shed. Aside from the abandoned oil tanks, there were no structures on my 160 acres, and I needed a structure. Oklahoma is subject to major storms with monster-size hail. Because of this every farmer in Oklahoma has a metal shed where they park vehicles and store equipment. I planned to build more substantial structures on the property later, but in the meantime, I needed a shed. I asked Farmer Phil for a recommendation, and he obliged kindly without mention of our previous conversation.

Days later a man named Rob showed up to survey the land and talk to me about putting a metal shed on the property. He was around the same age as Farmer Phil and very chatty. Along with being friendly, people in Oklahoma are very interested in what you are doing, and it can seem nosy to someone from the Bay Area who isn't used to being asked personal questions until the fifth or tenth year of a relationship. In California, we like to chat and get to know people before we dig deeper. In Oklahoma, they don't waste time making small talk. Instead, they dive right into your personal business. Rob was less of a gentleman than Farmer Phil, and there was no beating around the bush with him.

THE WEATHER CHANNEL

One of Dr. Tatiana's new favorite genres on the Weather Channel is the weather in Oklahoma where they show pictures of kids in various helmets (football, bike, etc.) holding hail bigger than softballs up to the camera after a storm.

She also learned from the Oklahoma-based Weather Channel that in Oklahoma, they don't even call California-size hail, "hail." It's just sleet in Oklahoma. If it doesn't dent a truck, that's not "hail" in Oklahoma.

"You from California? You must be here to farm pot." Then he immediately went for the kill. "I guess you probably hate Trump, huh?"

My background as an entrepreneur has prepared me to deal with people from all walks of life. In general, successful businesspeople are good at this. We routinely deal with employees and customers from different backgrounds, ideologies, and motivations. What I've learned is that as different as we might appear or our lives might be, we all put our pants on one leg at a time, from the person who owns the business to the person who cleans the floors. This is important to remember when working with communities on environmental initiatives: Start from a place that looks for things that can unite rather than divide people and communities. I entered into the conversation with Rob coming from this perspective. We likely had more in common than not.

Unfortunately people are divided now more than ever. We have labeled one another and picked a team in an us-versus-them mentality, and we tend to approach interactions with an offense-is-the-best-defense strategy. Rather than taking the Trump bait that Rob was dangling assuredly in front of me, you'll see in a moment how in response to him (and all similar aggression and confrontational questions that are hoping to pigeonhole me into some stereotype), I used my limited knowledge of improv: "Yes, and ..."

The idea in improv, rather than winning a conversation, is to make room for the other players on the stage to continue the act.

As such the rules are simple: Absorb, accept, add. Essentially always say, "Yes, and ..." I have modified this to some degree:

Don't take the bait and respond in defense or retaliation.

Take the time to listen, really listen, and try to understand what the other person is saying and where they are coming from.

I never answer a question directly and allow the other person the opportunity to judge; instead, I ask a question in return to keep the conversation going.

Assume the best, meaning that, until proved otherwise, believe that the other person has good intentions.

Sympathize and empathize with other perspectives.

Be willing to make a joke at my own expense to allow for a connection.

My aim is to get the other person talking and to evolve the conversation so that I can understand his or her true perspective and motivations.

"You from California?" Rob asked.

"Are there a lot of people coming here from California?" I returned the question.

"Heaps. Tons from California. I guess you hate Trump?"

"What do you think of Trump?"

"I voted for him. So I guess you're here to farm pot?"

"Is that a big industry out here?"

"Sure. People come from California to farm pot. It's changing the whole farming industry and disrupting the community."

With that line he revealed his real concern, and we had a base from which to launch a genuine conversation.

MY FAVORITE JOKES ABOUT MISCOMMUNICATION

I got into some trouble at the grocery store. When the lady at the register said strip down facing me, it turns out she was talking about my credit card.

Abbot and Costello's "Who's on First"
Abbot: I'm telling you. Who's on first, What's on Second, I Don't Know is on third.
Costello: You know the fellows' names?
Abbot: Yes.
Costello: Well, then who's playing first?
Abbot: Yes.

Let's eat, Grandpa vs. Let's eat Grandpa!

Scary Words in Oklahoma

I had the opportunity to call on Farmer Phil's offer of help yet again when I decided that I wanted the oil tanks removed from my property. Again Farmer Phil was willing to help, although all of my neighbors said this was impossible to get anyone from the oil industry to remove their equipment. In decades of trying, they had never succeeded. But as with the tractor tire, I was both naïve and determined. Farmer Phil helped me get in contact with the oil guy. Turns out I could have simply read the sign next to the derricks on my property (complete with the phone number), but I was still a slow learner.

Every conversation that I'd had in Oklahoma had involved scary words, but I really worried that things were headed in a bad direction when I met with Brian from the oil company. Brian started with the standard line of questioning about my being from California—likely there to sell pot and not a Trump supporter. I fell into my "Yes, and…" routine.

"You may not appreciate the oil industry," Brian said to me then.

"I don't know anything about it," I said honestly. "Tell me about it."

"I can tell you we're fighting some wars about it," he said.

It ended up that Brian was a veteran who had served in several wars in the Middle East. He told me a few stories about being involved in the conflicts. Then he told me a story about being home. "The other day I went into the 7-Eleven. My friend was walking out as I was walking in, and he said to me, 'Don't you go in there. There's a towelhead working there. He owns the store. You don't need to spend your money on some towelhead. I'm going to go back in there and kick his ass.'"

"Wow," I said, because I didn't know what to say. The story was getting quickly uncomfortable, and I wasn't sure if I should listen or try to change the subject. But before I could make a decision, Brian went on.

"I told my neighbor I had fought in many, many wars to make it possible for that towelhead to run that store, and I was ready to fight another one if he wasn't going to allow this man to make a living."

"Wow," I said again, this time meaning it. "What was his response?"

"My friend thanked me for my service, shut his mouth, and walked away."

"I imagine you never considered being in the military," Brian said to me then.

"No. Guns and violence are not my thing, but I deeply respect your service."

He nodded. "Don't you worry. I'll have those oil rigs off your property in ten minutes."

None of my neighbors could believe it. "How did you get him to do that?" they asked.

I had listened and understood. Together Brian and I had realized that there was more sameness in the ways that we viewed the world than difference.

A Second Chance

I arranged to meet a second time with Farmer Phil. I had learned some things about farming and farmers in Oklahoma in the meantime, and I was better prepared. This time Farmer Phil and I stood in a field under the sun and started a conversation that went on for hours until I could feel a sunburn blooming on my face. Like all the other conversations that I'd had in Oklahoma since first talking to Farmer Phil, it was extraordinarily and shockingly positive.

"This is what I really want to do," I leveled with Farmer Phil. "I want to get to a place where farmers can be stewards of the land. You are so knowledgeable about things like soil, ecosystems, and the environment. You are in a perfect position to make change. Why can't we do that?"

"Young lady," Farmer Phil said, "farmers are the only stewards of the land. Who do you think takes care of this entire earth?"

It seemed Farmer Phil's understanding was limited to the farm fields of Oklahoma. He didn't see the bigger picture. "What about the oceans and the forest and the rest?" I pointed.

Again Farmer Phil proved that my perception of him was wrong. His words, stated so simply, concealed the richness of the thought behind them. He had considered all of what I was thinking, and more. He was not one step behind me but two steps ahead. "Farmers care for those too. I think of all those caretakers as farmers," he said. He explained the intimate knowledge of the geography, geology, topography, weather, and intricacies of the environments that all these

82

people had to clearly understand in order to interact them successfully. "Who do you think cares about this planet more than farmers do? Farmers' lives depend directly upon it."

It was true. Stewardship was broader than I had previously considered and had many more applications than I had given it credit for.

"Could we find some way to grow food without damaging the thing we love?" I asked, because now I knew that if someone could find a solution to this problem, it was likely Farmer Phil.

"We absolutely could," Farmer Phil agreed. "I have seventy-five different ways to do that. You think I don't know that when I'm using pesticides, it's bad for the environment?

MANY KINDS OF FARMERS

- Dairy (cows for milk)
- Poultry (chickens and other birds for eggs and meat)
- Ranch (grazing livestock)
- Vineyard (wine)
- Orchard (fruit and nut trees)
- Apiary (bees)
- Aquaculture (fish, shellfish, aquatic plants, etc.)

I know it. I don't want to use them, but I have to feed my family, and so I need the crop to succeed. If you can tell me another way to farm so that I can still feed my family, I am all ears."

Across the board, this was what I heard from farmers: "I am hungry for a new way of doing things. If you've got an idea, I want to hear it. I don't care if you're from California and have never been a farmer. I want to hear your good idea." They were desperate to escape the current paradigm. It was ruining them not only financially but also psychologically and emotionally. Till farming goes against their intuition. Farming conditions have become soul crushing, and farmers are willing to try anything that will allow them to survive while still maintaining who they are and their family identity, farming.

Across the board, when I speak to clients, employees, business-people, and industry leaders about making changes to positively affect the climate, this is also what I hear: "I am hungry for a new way of doing things." People want to act in responsible ways that make them feel good, they want to create and live in a healthier world, they want to find and implement new solutions. People can get sidetracked by or focused on terms, ideologies, or labels, but when you shift the conversation away from these, you often make room for people to generate and share ideas.

As Rainmaker Farm grew and progressed, the farmers in the community would drive by to witness the transition (or the circus as we learned from our mistakes). It was amusing even if it was not yet informative. They would stop, chat, and ask if they could help out in any way. That's part of the farming culture in Oklahoma but also they wanted to see it with their own eyes and know if something else was possible.

My education in Oklahoma went well beyond farming; it reinforced my belief that people are more the same than we are different. What appears at the outset to be differences are often only different reactions motivated by the same things or are the same ideas manifest in different ways. In the end, we are all people working to make a living, raise children, protect and provide for our families; we are passionate about many of the same things. We have to stop thinking in terms of us versus them. The labels that we use to group one another simplify complex situations and only serve to box one another in and prevent communication. And communication is important. It ignites unity, cooperation, collaboration, and mutual understanding, all of which are beneficial to people and businesses trying to get things done. We can get on the same page if we start truly seeing one another as individuals. Unity is the key to solving problems related to climate change

Also I was reminded that it's important to look and work outside of our bubbles. Climate change issues are global issues. Solving problems related to climate change will demand that we reach beyond our bubbles and communicate with those who are different from us socially, economically, and philosophically. This shouldn't be scary; it should be exciting. Ultimately I've learned that I am richer for having learned about and listened to people who look at things differently than I do. I am never sorry that I listened and engaged with individuals who have different life experiences and who view the world differently than me. And I don't need to cross the country to do it. I can find other ways of thinking in my office, while out buying groceries, and around the corner, all I need is curiosity and a willingness to listen. I genuinely believe that you can learn something new from each person you speak with each time you speak with them. At the very least, by engaging with other people, I almost always end up with a good story.

Take Action: Communicate

Communication is a necessary part of solving the world's climate change issues, and communication is complicated. In order to communicate genuinely and effectively, you must respect those involved in the conversation, learn to listen, and find ways to deliver your message that can be understood and accepted. Here are some practical things you can do:

Tier 1: The Savvy At-Home Composter

1. Consider any and all conversations with **everyone** you speak with an opportunity to learn something.
2. Seek out and talk to people who think differently than you; ask them honestly what led them to their conclusions; learn from their answers.
3. Talk to your children about their experiences and fears in the world; it will likely move you to learn from them and implement their ideas in some ways.
4. Travel; get out of your local area to find more folks with more perspectives.
5. As an employee of a company, use your voice to communicate with company leaders to affect change.
6. Talk to your family and friends about what you are doing and what you have learned.

Tier 2: The CEO Environmental Powerhouse

1. Open dialogs within your companies. Make office communications more conversational (they don't always need to be about the bottom line or this quarter's earnings). This style of inclusion allows for more creative problem-solving and thus creates more effective organizations. This is the type of platform you need to build to begin big conversations about climate change and ESG, and you just might get a few new money-making ideas from employees who feel comfortable communicating.
2. Also take the Tier 1: Savvy At-Home Composter actions.

Tier 3: The Big Cheese World Changer

1. Communicate with world leaders, the ultimate negotiation, the triple win.

2. Standard negotiation tactics dictate that understanding the position of the other person drives leverage.

3. You earned your position and power by being open-minded but singularly purposed; use that skill when communicating with others—allow for the presentation to be limited and opinionated at first, and then watch how it changes as the communication continues.

4. Also take the Tier 2: CEO Environmental Powerhouse actions.

5. Also take the Tier 1: Savvy At-Home Composter actions.

CHAPTER 4

Global Is Local

The Local Weather Report and the Corner Grocery Store

These days most people I know catch the weather report sporadically. We watch it like a soap opera when unbelievable environmental events are occurring, and at all other times disregard it. It seems to have little impact when it isn't causing an adrenaline rush. The prominence of heating and cooling large indoor stadiums and other facilities sometimes make it feel like we can control the weather. We forget that the weather is always in charge.

EXCEPT DR. TATIANA

...who will drive anyone nuts with play-by-play updates of pending weather patterns on a very regular basis, including summaries of how said weather patterns are influenced by global circulation patterns and what this means for wildlife and humanity's future. Way to be a bright spot, Dr. Tat!

Since becoming a farmer, however, I have also become more attuned to the weather. I especially watch weather in Oklahoma daily and keep track of rainfall, temperature, and other things that affect crops.

When I was a kid, people of my grandparents' generation used to read or listen to the daily weather report. What they wanted to know was very specific: What would the weather be in their community the following day? They wanted to know if rain would interrupt their plans and what temperatures they should be dressing for. They didn't care about tornadoes two states over or the cold winter that was coming in a few months' time due to storms currently raging in Asia. Their concerns were immediate and local.

ANOTHER THING DR. TATIANA AND I AGREE ON *(AN ODE TO GROCERY STORES)*

The beauty and luxurious abundance of grocery stores. We love wandering through the produce aisle, filled with the rich smells of veggies and fruit, the delicate mist that makes it all look pretty, even the looks we get from other patrons as we squeeze, shake, and inhale. When COVID ended, Dr. Tatiana and I ditched the delivery services that had kept our pantries stocked (those rebound affairs we'd needed in the interim) and returned to our first love, where we could stroll the aisles and pick whatever looked good.

Even though we now get Arabic language shows on Netflix, watch YouTube videos from Central Africa, and see news that pays attention to global issues, our concerns are often still as immediate as those of our grandparents' generation: What is going to affect me right here, right now? (Basically, do I need to bring an umbrella?) We don't often ask what causes these effects or think about daily issues on a grander scale. This is true not only for things going on around us but for the origins of things in our own homes.

Let's talk about food. I'm a grocery girl. I don't buy shoes, I buy groceries. The grocery store is what the daytime talk shows (I can't really watch) would call "my happy place." I love everything about it. I like the little cart that you get to push around, the bins of produce that you can pick through, the aisles of boxed whatnots. I love all the choices and the smells and the weird lighting. I like the strolling pace and the odd encounters with strangers.

Dr. Tatiana and I also agree on the glory of farmer's markets.

I routinely walk by the meat counter and look at all the carcasses hanging on display in the background. It's amazing how many dead chickens, cows, and pigs they have—the supply of meat for my local area for maybe a week. There are probably no less than fifty grocery stores in the surrounding area, and every one of them has a similar display. In the next town over, there are another fifty grocery stores and another fifty displays. It's a tremendous amount of food. My mind begins to wander. What if it all doesn't get sold? And where did all those animals come from?

Almost no one else is wondering: Where does all this food come from? Instead we are thinking: Why are the free-range eggs so much more expensive than the regular ones? Why is my local shop always out of the bread with the oats on the crust? The grocery store (at least in wealthy areas; food deserts in economically disadvantaged areas are a problem) is like a table of opulence at a modern Roman banquet. You can get a hundred different kinds of anything you want. It's over the top. We can go into a grocery

---

FUNNY STORY FROM DR. TATIANA

I overheard a phone conversation at my grandmother's house in Michigan when I was about fourteen years old talking to an unknown friend about someone else's dietary preferences:

"She's a vegetarian?"

Pause.

"No! She doesn't even eat fish?"

Pause.

"No. Not even if it's from a can?"

ACCORDING TO MERRIAM WEBSTER

"Food desert: an area where little fresh produce is available for sale."[36]

---

36   Merriam-Webster.com Dictionary, s.v. "food desert," accessed May 23, 2023, https://www.merriam-webster.com/dictionary/food%20desert.

store at any time of the year and get raspberries: Summer—raspberries, local drought—raspberries, snowing outside—raspberries. Where do these raspberries come from? I imagine someone from a place like Sudan, where she might carry water for five miles from the well to her home, now finding herself in my local grocery store. The shock. The horror. Many of my children's friends think that the chicken their parents buy in the grocery is not the same kind of chicken they sing about living happily on the farm ("a cluck cluck here …").

It isn't only our food source from which we are disconnected. We don't know from where most of our essential and unessential goods come: electricity, gasoline, flip-flops, jeans, and toothpaste. We go to the sink, turn the tap, and out comes water. Magic. Obviously water comes from the sink. We don't think about the Colorado River drying up, which will not only deplete our supply of drinking water but also the electricity that the river generates and the food from the farmland it irrigates. When the water stops flowing, we'll call the plumber. When the lights go out, we'll call our utility provider.

MY PET CHICKENS

I have chickens at my house. I don't slaughter them, although I do steal their eggs. Mostly, I like to look at them. They make my lawn look pretty. But inevitably, something else eats your chickens (raccoons, coyotes. Eagles are what you hope for because they just pick up the chicken and it disappears without making a mess). Chickens are disposable, and you have to replenish the stock every couple of years. I waited until my kids were four or five before I let them really experienced the carnage. Then we had a talk about the circle of life. That's how I introduced my kids to meat.

Last year Rainmaker Farm had its first wheat harvest, and I not only learned a lot about growing wheat but also a lot about what happens to wheat after it's grown. It turns out that the US exports wheat to Mexico, the Philippines, China, Japan, and South Korea and imports wheat from Canada, Poland, Italy, Mexico (we are apparently passing wheat back and forth with our southern neighbor), and the United Kingdom.[37] I had previously assumed that anything grown in the Midwest stayed there.

It made me think differently about the grocery store. We grow things in the US (bell peppers, tomatoes, grapes), but if you look closely, you'll likely see stickers on these that say "Product of Guatemala" or a host of other places. And these are the unrefined products. Processed foods that combine many ingredients, like bread with oats on the crust for example, can involve harvests from several other countries.

On its own the shipment of food across borders directly and indirectly works to put carbon dioxide into the air, but it is also one example of a larger issue that we face when trying to make a positive impact on the environment. We often function on all three tiers (at home, as CEOs, and as industry leaders) on automatic pilot. We go along with what is happening and has always happened without truly examining or understanding the systems in which we function and upon which we depend. When we begin to pick them apart, we find that they are far more complex than we imagined, and maybe more complex than they need to be.

---

37   The Multidimensional Economic Complexity Ratings, "Wheat in United States," OEC, February 2023, https://oec.world/en/profile/bilateral-product/wheat/reporter/usa.

In the Weeds

Wheat was one of the first crops I planted at Rainmaker Farm as part of our transition from conventional to no-till, regenerative farming. Previously the farm had exclusively been a red winter wheat crop farm. I was planning multiculture rather than monoculture farming, meaning that I was going to plant many crops that would work together throughout the year to replenish the soil. But I also wanted to model regenerative farming utilizing crops that are regularly grown in the area so that I was successful in a crop, and language, the local farmers could relate to. After all they were the community I was trying to reach with my ideas and example of regenerative farming.

Rainmaker Farm is small with only a few sizeable fields that are between twenty and forty acres each. Last year, I dedicated one of them to the red winter wheat. The first thing that I had to do was buy seed—some strains are thought to do better with no-till farming. Then I had to find a no-till drill-planting machine for rent.

A point of annoyance for me was that I also needed to purchase and organize the distribution of fertilizer to my new crop. I would have preferred not to have used fertilizer, but if you are cultivating crops and taking them off site, then nutrients are leaving your farm, making fertilizing a necessity. While researching fertilizers, I learned that most of the fertilizer used by farmers in the US comes from places like Russian and China. (Sounds a little like the grocery store, right?) I learned this about the time that China was considering imposing a ban on importing US trash, something we had been sending them for years. It seemed ironic that we were shipping them our trash and buying their shit. Another reason I was bitter about having to buy fertilizer is that a truly regenerative farm incorporates livestock, providing the farm with its own fertilizer. It's a lot cheaper to manage grazing "meat cows" than to purchase fertilizer, but I did not yet have grazing cows and was not yet producing my own fertilizer. Instead of having my own cow manure, I had to buy chicken shit from another farm to fertilize my wheat crop. My neighbor Matt (another seventh-generation farmer) told me that if I didn't fertilize, I wouldn't get a good crop.

Matt is a little younger than me and has a bachelor of science in plant and soil sciences from Oklahoma State University. He is a young, smart farmer who is really excited about the Rainmaker Farm project and my transition from a conventional to a no-till farm, something he has been implementing on some of his land. Like nearly every farmer in the area, he is married to a teacher, and like every farmer in the area, he constantly and sincerely offers his assistance. I had needed his assistance quite a few times. He had been working a great deal with Rainmaker Farm, helping us to prepare and plant fields. I also rented his equipment. Matt had a no-till drill and a manure spreader.

MANURE-SPREADER JOKES *(I CAN'T RESIST)*

What happens when you run out of manure on a farm?

You have to make doo.

Today while I was driving, I saw a manure truck tipped over.

I guess you could say that guy lost his shit.

The tractor company's manure spreader is the only piece of equipment they won't stand behind.

Every year the Manure Expo runs a public competition for "crappy slogans." I love that they have a sense of humor (a sense of humor is advantageous when trying to communicate). In 2023, the top submissions were:

- A Super-Spreader Event
- Where Talking Shit Is Cool
- Manure Haulers: Spreading the Wealth
- The World's Biggest Gathering of Turd Nerds
- Manure Happens. We Make the Most of It
- The Allure of Manure
- Rated "M" for Manure
- You Name the Species, We've Got the Feces
- If You're Squeamish About Poo, This T-shirt's Not For You
- We've Always Been Socially Distant

Fertilizing, planting, and harvesting fields are momentous tasks that take hours. Whole families get involved in shifts—spouses, kids, grandparents—working together to put in eighteen-hour days during the busy season, keeping the machinery running constantly to get the job done. It isn't unusual for a ten-year-old to know how to run a tractor or for an eighty-year-old to still be driving one. Everyone gets involved.

One thing I did refuse to do was use pesticides. The land has been violated on numerous levels—oil extraction, tilling, and pesticides. I wanted to let the soil rest and recover. I had planned to let the farm run fallow but decided to plant the wheat as a learning experience. I needed to get the hang of farming, or at least figure out what I needed to learn. But the lack of pesticides meant that when my crop came up, weeds came up as well, a lot of weeds, which ultimately degraded the quality of my harvest. This was anticipated. I'd known the risk when I decided to opt out of the pesticides. But the weeds were worse than I'd expected.

"Should have used pesticides," the other farmers said.

I started using my entrepreneurial skills and began coming up with solutions to my weed problem. Could I companion plant something that would kill the weeds? Could I mow it? The farmers with whom I talked shook their heads and said in different ways, "You're screwed." I couldn't mow eight thousand acres. That was ridiculous. They were right.

"You're never going to kill that weed," other farmers told me. "That's horseweed, and it just doesn't kill even with pesticides."

"What? Hold on a second," I said. "There's a hole in your story, my friend. Pesticide wouldn't have prevented this anyway?"

Pesticides wouldn't kill or prevent horseweed, other farmers told me, only diminish it. While not using pesticides may have made my situation worse in terms of weeds, it had certainly not caused the issue.

TILL VS. NO-TILL

Tilling wreaks havoc on the soil. It literally tears it up and inhibits the soil's ability to sequester carbon.

However, tilling also inhibits weeds, which is one of the reasons farmers till, especially in situations when they are not using pesticides.

I accepted that I was stuck with weeds for the harvest, but they stuck around after I harvested my wheat crop when I planted a soil-building cover crop that included oats and grasses. Everything grew: the oats, the grasses, and the weeds. They were all getting tall. "There's got to be something I can do with this," I said. Again I heard from fellow farmers that cover crops were a waste of time, and there was nothing to be done with or about either the cover crops or the weeds.

I started coming up with ideas. Sometimes farmers burn their land, a process that seems apocalyptic but is a natural and integral process that releases nutrients in old grasses and regenerates soil to some degree. Or what if I grazed it? Or baled it and fed it to animals?

VOCAB: COVER CROPS

Cover crops are crops that you plant to protect the soil between growing the crops that will harvest. Cover crops add nutrients to and replenish the soil after it has been depleted by growing or tilling. You choose cover crops according to the type of soil that you have and what that soil is missing or needs.

Field:

- Turnip
- Radish
- Winter Pea
- Barley
- Winter Oat
- Common Vetch

"I wouldn't feed that to my cattle," a neighboring farmer told me.

He wouldn't, but maybe someone would. Maybe I could sell it and make enough money to cover the cost of the seed and labor it took to grow it in the first place, making it an economically viable initiative.

Matt weighed in on this. "You could sell that baled," he said, "but only to feed lots."

Feed lots, ironically, were the exact opposite of what I was working toward. Feed lots take cattle off the land where they graze and fertilize the soil and cram them onto concrete slabs where they eat all day and fart methane. (Most feed lots in Oklahoma are only a temporary holding place for cows on their way to slaughter.) But Matt was right, feed lots didn't care what they fed the animals so long as it was cheap. They might pay me a couple of bucks a bale.

A week later I was in Texas where there was also a terrible drought. I heard some ranchers saying they may need to slaughter their cattle because they couldn't feed them. Bingo. I was in the right place at the right time with the right resource. "Are you looking for a particular kind of hay?" I asked. "Because I've got these weeds that I can bale."

This rancher lit up. "I'll take anything. I don't care if it's got sticks and rocks in it. I'll buy it. I've got nothing, and nobody's growing anything around here."

I told him that I had just mowed some fields with oat and rye (and lots of weeds).

"I'd pay for that," he said.

Everybody wins. The rancher gets cheap food for his cattle. I make a little money. The conversation happened in great part by chance. In the future, I will know to look beyond my local market.

The thing about people is that when we are caught up in our everyday lives, we don't tend to look beyond what is familiar and immediate—the place we always get coffee or where we always shop. Farmers have their established contacts and established way of doing things. Further, although currently attempting to be a farmer, I still had an entrepreneurial mindset, which is about innovation and imagining possibilities. I was willing to entertain all ideas, even those that were impractical—which goes against the philosophy that drives most farmers—and that meant I had possibilities and created opportunities.

This also applies to businesses. Successfully transforming a company or industry into one that has a positive environmental impact requires creativity, innovation, and thinking about things in a new way that allows you to see possibilities and create opportunities. Stepping outside of my comfort zone to become a farmer reminded me that the entrepreneurial mindset is a great asset. We need to be able and willing to consider unconventional ideas that lead to inventive solutions, and we need to be able to convince others to do the same.

Farmers are often focused on getting the high yield for the least amount of effort and cost. If they look at a situation and estimate that it will take tons more effort but only generate the same yield, they won't do it. This is my biggest fight with farmers. The only way that I will be able to convince them to put in more effort is to prove that it will make them more money, which means that through Rainmaker Farm, I need to make more money than they do.

For me Rainmaker Farm is about proving the merits of regenerative farming, but more than that, it is about leading through example, taking the risks myself, and offering real, tangible proof that actions

HOMEWORK

Watch *Kiss the Ground*

and initiatives that are environmentally conscious are also good for business. I try to do this across the board with all the actions and initiatives for which I advocate, from Tier 1 through Tier 3. Environmentally conscious initiatives often demand an initial investment that does not pay back immediately, but in the long term, they are not only worth it but necessary. Conducting business from an environmentally conscious standpoint is necessary for the survival of your business, and changing the farming industry to be more regenerative is necessary for continued production.

A Little Education: Old MacDonald Had a Fiscal Policy

In order to truly understand the decisions that farmers make, you first need to understand the way that farming works, the fiscal policies that affect farming, and the pressures these policies put on farmers. Consider a best-case scenario: First you, the farmer, ready the field, which for most farmers means tilling, fertilizing, and spreading pesticides. This requires you to purchase fertilizer and pesticide at market value and obtain (likely rent) equipment and possibly pay employees to run that machinery. Market value fluctuates wildly at the whims of weather, political conflicts, worldwide inflation, etc. Let's say that you happen to need fertilizer and pesticide at a time when the market price is low.

INCREASING YOUR VOCABULARY: DRY FARMING

In Oklahoma, most farmers don't irrigate. This is a process called dry farming. They rely entirely on rain.

Let's also say that rather than renting machinery (the cost for buying new machines ranges between half a million and a million dollars), you have a legacy machine, passed down through generations, that you have become skilled at repairing on your own (farmers are, by necessity, jacks-of-all-trades). Once you ready your field, you buy seed, also at market value, and use another machine (that you rent or own) to plant. Then you wait for months and months. You watch the weather and hope for just enough rain, but not too much. If you are a person with certain beliefs, you might pray. You wait for six months until your crop has grown and is ready to harvest.

Let's say that because you used pesticides, you don't have a lot of weeds. Because you fertilized well, you have a high-yield crop, meaning it is healthy and there's lots of it. Now you rent/borrow/own a combine that harvests your crop and (this is where that famous phrase comes from) separates the wheat from the chaff and finally bring your crop to your local collection (grain elevator) and testing center where your crop is tested for quality. Based on the quality and amount of your crop, you are offered a price at market value on that day. Now you have a choice to make: You can sell your crop that day at the price offered or wait (and watch the commodity market, which is based off of geopolitics, weather, or any other stuff you don't control) and hope the price will go up, knowing that the price may also go down. It's a little like a game show, except it's your entire livelihood.

HOMEWORK FOR OVERACHIEVERS: WATCH CLARKSON'S FARM

...On Amazon Prime, a British documentary series wherein Jeremy Clarkson (host of Top Gear) buys a farm, gives up his city life for a season, and tries to grow stuff. Season 1, Episode 8 portrays Clarkson's first harvest and portrays well the nuts and bolts of harvesting a crop and the many pitfalls that can derail plans, including the rush to harvest the wheat while it remains within a certain dew point average that will keep it from growing mold.

Farming expertise is in agriculture, but farmers also have to be stockbrokers in order to succeed. They need to watch the prices of commodities, like fertilizer and pesticide. They need to predict the ways that political instability in the world will shift markets. They need to understand how a trade war with China will drive fertilizer prices. Or how a war in Ukraine might drive the price of wheat. Conversations between farmers have gone from weather to sanctions on Russia. Farmers are thinking about political conflicts from a stock market lens—this not their natural thing. But even with all this new awareness, farming is still a crap shoot. Every season they weigh the risks of investing tens of thousands of dollars—into fertilizer, pesticides, seed, equipment rental, gasoline to run that equipment, and labor—to grow a crop against the potential rewards, knowing they could see dramatic fluctuations in the market price before sale, local bad weather that ruins their crop, global weather events that interrupt trade, political instability, an insect infestation, or other acts of God.

This is where the government comes in. Starting in the early 1930s, the government began to offer farmers incentives to grow certain commodity crops by guaranteeing a set market price for that crop. Because grains are the crops that feed our world, these are the main crops that government programs support (wheat, corn, and soy). The good thing for the farmer is that growing crops supported by government subsidies takes some of the risk out of their endeavors, but it also pays farmers for certain crops even if there is not a market for those crops, violating the natural food economy. And the bad thing for farmers is that playing it safe and farming only a subsidized crop means that many multiculture farms that once invested in the production of several kinds of food are now monoculture farms that use GMO seed, pesticides, and other practices to increase the mass of their yield in the short term but also harm the land in the long term, diminishing the quality not only of the product but also of the farmer's land. This further handicaps the farmer, making it difficult for her to plant diverse crops that the soil can no longer support. It's a vicious cycle.

A NOTE FROM DR. TATIANA

That is the origin of marketplace—where food is bought and sold. Crops are (and always will be) the foundation of a global economy.

THE 1930S *(AKA "THE HANGOVER OF THE ROARING '20S")*

1929: Wall Street Market Crash leads to the Great Depression
1930: The Dust Bowl begins
1931: Food riots/banks collapsing
1933: The New Deal
1935: Works Progress Administration and USDA Soil Conservation Service instituted

If some of this language seems familiar to you, it also feels familiar to a lot of farmers. Words like "subsidies," "incentives," and "aid" are the same words used to describe government assistance programs. Farmers talk about these government programs as a kind of welfare.

Welfare is designed to help people when they get into a bind. But having known lots of people on welfare, what it does in practice is gives people, or guarantees people, the bare minimum. Because that is more than they were sometimes able to get in the past, it feels secure. They are trapped into doing the same things done in the past and earning the minimum. They don't want to take a risk and try something else, learn something new, or put in an effort that might result in a catastrophic uninsured loss.

This is the way that till farming not only degrades the land but also the farmers who care for it. Farmers are barely getting by or not getting by at all. Many farmers who I know have mortgaged the land that has been in their families for generations to cover their costs and are working to buy back that land.

UNFUN FARM FACTS

According to the National Ag Safety Database, in the past 150 years, the percentage of people in the US involved in farming has decreased from 50 percent to 2 percent.[38]

Another unhappy statistic from the National Ag Safety Database, the stress of farming has led farmers to have a high rate of depression that leads to drug and alcohol abuse, violence, and suicide.

Returning to regenerative multiculture, no-till farming would solve many of these issues. Multiculture farming is a business-savvy model. Growing more than one crop is a way for farmers to diversify and hedge their bets, de-risking. If the weather conditions are bad this year and the wheat harvest sucks, your apple orchard might hit

---

38   *Depression: Common for Farm People*, NASD. (n.d.), https://nasdonline.org/7122/d002366/depression-common-for-farm-people.html.

the jackpot. This is not to mention that planting companion crops naturally enriches the soil, boosting the overall yield and quality of crops. If farmers also incorporate livestock, they not only add another product to sell, but they also get free fertilizer, lowering their upfront costs. Livestock that is allowed to graze on fields produces healthier meat because it is not crowded in feed lots that breed disease, meaning the animals that graze in fields require less vaccines and other medications to keep them alive. Regenerative farming not only offers more security, but also it's more lucrative. It's really a no-brainer. But change is difficult.

It is important to understand the role of global markets and governments in the farming industry because these larger forces, along with others, play a role in all industries where we need to enact change to globally get to net-zero carbon dioxide emissions. In order to truly change the actions of people en masse, we need to change policies, create incentives at the federal level, and get large institutions and whole industries on board with transforming their behavior to become environmentally conscious.

Farm to Table and Ukraine to Texas

The world is global. People shopping in their neighborhood grocery stores are more likely to be informed about major international issues than about the food they are buying, where it has come from, and the process it has gone through. What customers, like me, see are shortages and price increases that range from annoying and inconvenient to detrimental. Those changes at the grocery store, of course, are influenced by the farming industry, which is impacted not only by international political situations but also global climate events and a long history of policies that shape trade with other countries.

When Putin invaded Ukraine, I was in my backyard super-soaking one of my chickens who dared to step foot on my deck. During the month previous, I had been lightly watching the Olympics and enjoying the winter weather. When the news announced the first Russian tanks crossing Ukrainian borders, most people were probably thinking of bloodshed and terrible acts of violence. I was not only cursing the human race for causing exactly this but additionally considering wheat. Ukraine is a breadbasket of Europe—one of the largest wheat producers in the world. If they are at war, they are likely not growing wheat, which means the wheat supply will go down, and prices will go up.

TRAINING CHICKENS

My free-range chickens are allowed to go anywhere they want, except the deck, because I welcome their chicken shit fertilizer all over my lawn but not on the treated wood. Anyone who tells you that chickens cannot be trained has never lived with chickens. My chickens have learned that they are not allowed on the deck. I have trained them using one tool, a super-soaker that I purchased and keep on hand for exactly this purpose. Perhaps my next book will be a complete guide to training chickens, although the essential information is contained in this paragraph.

I was also imagining the dominos of later effects falling, one leading to another. The war will displace people resulting in intense immigration, first to neighboring countries, and then elsewhere. Imagine doubling the size of your town in a day, or even increasing it by 10 percent. There will be a new strain on resources, and the cycle will repeat as people continue to compete for oil, food, land, cattle, and all the resources people have been fighting over throughout human history.

Actions, like war or even government subsidies, set off a chain of reactions that inevitably have global bearing. This is the Butterfly Effect: The butterfly flaps its wings making a little breeze that builds and builds, and I'm now waiting for the resulting hurricane to hit continents away.

No Pain, No Grain

I wasn't off to a great start. I didn't have high expectations for the first year after the transition to no-till farming, and my first year farming, and those low expectations came true. My wheat crop was paltry. We were experiencing the worst US drought in over a hundred years, resulting in widespread crop failure. However, this was in part also my fault. I had chosen not to use pesticides, and this meant my field was weedier than it would have been had I used pesticides. But part of this was also the fault of Matt's manure spreader. It had done a "shitty" job evenly spreading the chicken litter. Looking out at the field, I could see where the manure spreader had successfully fertilized and where it had missed entire areas. Matt conceded that his manure spreader must not have been working very well that day.

The end result was a low yield when it came time to harvest. Matt ran the combine and didn't even harvest all the rows of wheat. They were just too weedy, and the cost of his time and renting the equipment would not have been covered by what I may have earned from the crop.

In the end I only harvested five or ten acres, which was devastating to some degree. However, watching the combine work was still quite an event. It's a tanklike truck pushing a wide, sharp, metal comb that pulls up the wheat, separates it from the chaff, and spits it out a shoot into an open trailer pulled alongside.

COMBINES ARE COOL

If you have ever seen the Disney movie Cars, the combine plays the monstrous bad guy when the cars are racing in somebody's field. It looks like a combination of a factory on wheels and a Medieval torture device. If you haven't seen a combine, it is worth looking up on Google images. Here are some shots I took.

Although my wheat crop was minimal at best, I decided to partake in the full experience and sell what I had. Matt put my wheat in a semi truck and drove it to be weighed at the grain elevator. After it was weighed, they took a sample and performed a quality test that included sorting out the weeds and grasshoppers to figure out what percentage of my harvest was actually wheat and then running the actual wheat through a dozen machines that poked and prodded it, like an annual exam for grain. There was even a point when the lady going through my sample got out a pair of tweezers and picked through parts of my sample by hand. At the end, a little machine printed out a receipt—not unlike the kind you would get at the grocery store—which seemed incredibly anticlimactic.

FACTS AND FIGURES: TESTING WHEAT

"The properties of grain quality can be summarized into ten main factors: (i) Uniform moisture content, (ii) High test weight, (iii) No foreign material, (iv) Low percentage of discolored, broken and damaged kernels, (v) Low breakability, (vi) High milling quality, (vii) High protein and oil content, (viii) High viability, (ix) No aflatoxin (mycotoxin), and (x) No presence of insects and molds."[39]

After the machines calculated the quality and quantity of my wheat, the truck was moved forward onto a structure. The belly of the truck opened. I watched my wheat fall into a massive dark hole of death that looked like it went straight through the earth.

"Where's it going?" I asked, staring into the abyss.

THE BEST THING ABOUT GETTING AN ACCOUNT AT THE GRAIN ELEVATOR

Me: I got to sell my grain, get close to some huge machinery, talk like a farmer to other farmers, and stare into the massive hole of death that simultaneously terrified me and made me want to jump in.

Dr. Tatiana: Access to daily market updates about how the price of grain in the rural areas is being influenced by global events and weather patterns.

Below was a system of conveyer belts that moved the grain into grain elevators. "Does it mix with everybody else's wheat? Where is it going now?"

Not only do consumers have no idea where our food comes from, but farmers also have no idea where their specific harvest goes, and in many cases, we have no idea how our food is created or from what.

39 Wikimedia Foundation, "Grain Quality," Wikipedia, December 23, 2022, https://en.wikipedia.org/wiki/Grain_quality.

The people at the market yard were very kind in allowing me to move through the whole process. They told me that many of the crops they'd seen had just as many weeds and said several times, "I'm really surprised that your harvest is as high equality as it is. It looked like it was going to be a lot worse." They explained the readings and the deficiencies of my crop without ridiculing. They were caring and sensitive without patronizing. I realized when they handed me the final ticket that they knew at the beginning of the process, although I did not, that my wheat crop was likely worth less than $500. There had been drought. Oklahoma had seen temperatures above 110°F. Other farmers were also bringing in entire crops worth only $500, and that was their entire income for the year.

Not Just Any Drought— The Worst in 100 Years

Once you have your receipt that states the quantity and quality of wheat, you go home with instructions to call the grain buyer when you want to sell. The grain buyer reviews all the wheat markets in the world. The range in prices from day to day can be tremendous, so that one day it may be selling at $6, and the following day it may rise over 100 percent to $14. This is why farmers have become market analysts. They must check the commodities markets and decide when to sell. Will it go up tomorrow? But what if it goes down? What if Putin invades Ukraine? Maybe I should wait? They have to guess. And the amount of money that a farmer earns from a

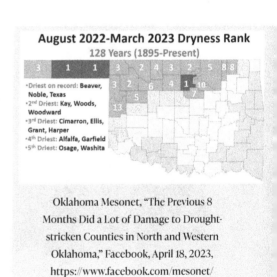

August 2022-March 2023 Dryness Rank
128 Years (1895-Present)

·Driest on record: **Beaver, Noble, Texas**
·2ⁿᵈ Driest: **Kay, Woods, Woodward**
·3ʳᵈ Driest: **Cimarron, Ellis, Grant, Harper**
·4ᵗʰ Driest: **Alfalfa, Garfield**
·5ᵗʰ Driest: **Osage, Washita**

Oklahoma Mesonet, "The Previous 8 Months Did a Lot of Damage to Drought-stricken Counties in North and Western Oklahoma," Facebook, April 18, 2023, https://www.facebook.com/mesonet/

harvest not only is that farmer's income, but it also determines what he or she will be able to invest in the following crop.

I asked Farmer Phil to tell me how the whole growing and selling a crop works. In a good year, meaning enough rain, good temperatures, no acts of God, etc., he spends about $10,000 on tilling and readying a farm of my size, another $10,000 buying and distributing seed and pesticide, and then sells his yield for $30,000.

CROP INSURANCE

Those farming in the standard way were eligible for, and likely had, crop insurance. Which, again, is why it is difficult to convince farmers to transition to my version of no-till regencrative farming.

All about crop insurance:

If you're a little slow on math, Farmer Phil would have made $10,000 in a good year on a field my size. $10,000. That's why 160 acres is a small farm in Oklahoma, and why hearing that a family farmer manages five thousand to twenty thousand acres isn't unusual

It was a sobering look at the wheat market. I needed a drink.

Farming involves great risk and so little reward that it's easy to see why farmers choose to grow subsidized crops. Because subsidized crops pay based on the amount and not the quality of the yield, farmers pull all the punches to produce as much as possible during the current harvest: pesticides, fertilizer, tilling, and prayer.

This works for a while.

But every season of monoculture, conventional farming depletes the soil so that next year more fertilizer and pesticides are required to maintain the same yield. It's like a drug that requires more and more to get the high each time. Or a Hollywood celebrity who has a little face-lift every year until finally their lips are pulled to their ears and they barely have a face anymore. It isn't sustainable. And farmers know it.

Something happens again and again when I speak to farmers in Oklahoma. They are excited about my project. They want to see me succeed. They want to hear my ideas. Farming is not easy and in some years not even profitable. They want their way of life to be sustainable and are open to new things.

I never got to taste my wheat. I mean, I took a couple of little nibbles at it and tried sticking some in my teeth and chewing on it the way you see farmers do on TV, but after it went into the black hole of death, I never knew where it went, or how it got milled, or what it became: Wonder Bread, pita, bacon jalapeño crackers, beer—I'd be proud of a good ale. It was a little sad, not so much not knowing what happened to my wheat, but that very definite way that I realized how impossible it was to be connected to the food chain. The world has gotten big ... or small. And although I don't know what happened to my wheat, and although I have no idea how cornflakes are made, when I eat breakfast, or anything else, I think of farmers.

SELL-DAY DRINK RECIPE

Crop the Top

1 part lemon juice

1 part grapefruit liqueur

1 part amaro

1 part gin

(Or whatever you have on hand)

Serve on ice

WHAT I WOULD NAME MY BEER

- Sweet Wheat Pale Ale
- Six Wheat Under Lager
- Wheat This! Punchy Pilsner
- Kiss My Wheat Porter

Take Action: Think Big

My experience with the wheat harvest is reflective of other global issues and especially global issues around climate change. In part it is because our world functions so globally rather than locally that it is difficult to see the causes and effects of particular actions. In the same way that I don't immediately associate the lack of Twinkies on the shelf at the grocery store to a wheat shortage two months ago in Europe, when refugees appear at our borders escaping war, they are so many steps removed from the change of weather patterns (that caused the drought that caused the depletion of farmland that caused a new fight for resources that caused war in their region), that we don't connect the dots. But it is fast becoming the case that all observable effects relate in some way to climate change.

It is also true that, like farming, we have created situations where doing the right thing seems or is immediately risky (like having a crop that cannot be insured because it is not farmed traditionally or making a decision to invest a great deal upfront into an environmentally conscious venture that won't have an immediate payoff or result), although in the long term these are the actions that might preserve our businesses. When we are worried about immediate survival, it is difficult, although necessary, to play the long game.

Climate change is a big, complex problem. It's not only going to take a forward-thinking view but also the acts of big entities to make changes in standards and policies. There are ways that you can help bring this about on all levels. Here are some things you can do to start understanding and intentionally shape your role in the global causes and effects of climate change, and some changes that you can make now that will help to shape your future:

Tier 1: The Savvy At-Home Composter

1. Buy local and not just food: But when at the grocery store, look to buy local food. That includes everything, not just produce. Your honey can be local (and some say can reduce allergies if you consume it). Your bread, milk, grains, and meat can all be local. Many grocery stores actually list when something is local to your area vs. not. If you live in a city, there are likely local farms just outside your area, and they are likely at farmer's markets on a scheduled basis. Buy from them, and while you're at it, talk to them. Guaranteed they will have interesting things to say.

2. When viewing your morning news source, consider where the conflicts you are reading about originate. Most conflicts large and small revolve around power, but what is power really? Its resources: food, land, energy, water, money, control of people to make money. Where is the "lack" in that conflict driving strife? Chances are it is prevalent in your area as well but to a lesser degree. For now, start to connect the dots around political instability and food sources. It's the easiest place to see it quickly.

3. Talk to your family and friends about what you are doing and what you have learned.

Tier 2: The CEO Environmental Powerhouse

1. Read Simon Sinek's *The Infinite Game*. It will benefit your business immediately. When you apply these strategies to a global perspective, further actions will become apparent in your industry and in your company.

2. Also take the Tier 1: Savvy At-Home Composter actions.

Tier 3: The Big Cheese World Changer

1. All industries have a breadcrumb trail of "backers," those who heavily invest (or invested) in capturing a market and controlling it. Often those backers are foreign countries both inside and outside of multinational trade agreements or politicians that side with big business perspectives to get elected. If your portfolio is large enough, you are likely aware of this and mitigate your risk of association with these backers either to promote opportunity or minimize loss. Look at these opportunities through an infinite game lens, consider the following, and make changes appropriately: Is your portfolio weighted to adjust when the players change? Will your successors be able to navigate the risks you balance in foreign affairs or with the politicians of the day? Like the farmers, will subsequent generations inherit unmanageable market conditions? Will the market structure you work within now still exist? Are the industries in your portfolio dying or adapting to an economic world based on resource scarcity climate response?

2. Also take the Tier 2: CEO Environmental Powerhouse actions.

3. Also take the Tier 1: Savvy At-Home Composter actions.

CHAPTER 5

A Low Carb(on) Diet

A Little Education: Drawdown

During the height of the COVID-19 pandemic, when everyone had been mostly home for months—not flying across the country or driving cars—we saw positive changes to the environment. The smog of pollution over major cities cleared, plants grew, people reported seeing wildlife that had disappeared from the areas for decades. The earth began to heal itself. We

DRAWDOWN

"Project Drawdown uses different scenarios to assess what determined, global efforts to address climate change might look like."[40]

Check out their solutions and scenarios here:

were certainly not experiencing drawdown (emissions barely dipped), but we were seeing light at the end of a long tunnel.

Climate drawdown will be achieved when the levels of greenhouse gas in our atmosphere not only stop rising but also begin to decline. This will eventually reduce the average global temperature increase and allow the earth to rebuild and begin to repair some of the damage that we have done. During the COVID-19 pandemic and international lockdown, the earth only saw about a 6.5 percent decrease in climate emissions. But even that small amount was enough to make noticeable changes.

---

40   *Table of Solutions*, Project Drawdown, (2021, August 16), https://drawdown.org/solutions/table-of-solutions.

Drawdown is absolutely doable if humanity gets on board with eliminating our carbon dioxide emissions from fossil fuels and recapturing carbon dioxide that is already in the atmosphere. This means we need to make choices to do and not do things according to how much carbon dioxide those activities will put into the atmosphere or back into the ground. Fundamentally we need to end our reliance on fossil fuels and plant a lot more to restore the living systems on earth to sequester carbon dioxide.

THE PLANTING TRIPLE WIN

Planting anything that grows is truly the first TANGIBLE thing I have found that has a measurable impact on the climate change problem. It's a triple win:

1. You can do it with your own hands (which means it doesn't need to cost you anything, and you reap the benefits of being involved in a physical outdoor activity).
2. You can scientifically measure the effects of your actions.
3. You can often eat the things your grow (or sell them).

* For the bonus, it can transform a landscape: create shade, block wind and sound, and even reverse desertification or create microclimates.

The development and use of clean energy technologies will be central to limiting the impacts of climate change as the world shifts away from emissions-intensive energy sources, and embracing clean energy alternative energy sources means fundamentally changing the way we produce and consume energy—in all its forms.

While the Tier 1 actions that you take—the solar panels on your house, the electric car you drive, and the limitations you put on your personal travel in combination with the garden in your backyard—all help with the world's decarbonization ambition, we really need to see change happen on a grander scale: with governments and industries. This is where Tier 3 participants need to step up to influence policy change, along with things like Environmental, Social, and Governance (ESG) criteria for businesses and other initiatives for specific industries. This is why CEOs, like myself, are in such a critical position during this major shift in our society and economy. Soon these types of measures will be required for transacting business or policy. Those who get ahead of these regulations and participate in their creation, report compliance, and get used to transacting in a new ecological economy will have a business advantage.

MY ELECTRIC CAR

Utilities and transportation industries are working to electrify EVERY-THING in coming years. Electric vehicles are not going away. Neary every car company now sells them.

Sometime ago, I found myself in a situation where I was going to be driving potentially eighty minutes a day. I drove a Lexus Rx that *I loved*, but it got twenty-four miles to the gallon. ☹ I like to keep cars for a minimum of a decade, but I knew I had to upgrade. That's when I got the Tesla.

It is IMMEDIATELY freeing to drive an emissions free car. Especially when it is not really a car at all but a full-blown spaceship. I have never looked back.

Except for this time when I actually tried to look back, through the back window to back up (old school driver-style: no camera). Apparently when I do that, my butt lifts up from the seat (I am short) and triggers the pressure sensors in the seat to SLAM THE CAR INTO PARK. It was not graceful. And of course it happened in front of lots of people.

The first step toward drawdown is switching from fossil fuels to low-carbon energy sources across all sectors. Electricity is one of the largest utilities in terms of global usage. Not only does electricity run the cappuccino machine that gets you going every morning, but it has also historically been pivotal to our growth as a society and is dramatically on the rise with the electrification of nearly all household and societal goods and services. However, the electricity industry is currently one of the largest contributors to global greenhouse gas emissions. This doesn't have to be the case. Electric utilities have a powerful opportunity to not only enable but also spearhead decarbonization at an economy-wide or even global level.

Utilities have been making strides to decarbonize for decades, reaching net-zero emissions in the short time frame necessary to avoid climate crisis catastrophe; however, it will take a paradigm shift. That shift may be coming. In 2022, the White House issued an executive order to accelerate the process to bring the electricity industry to net-zero emissions. The goal is for the electricity industry to be carbon free by 2035.[41]

$11 MILLION PER MINUTE

This is the amount, according to the International Monetary Fund, that the fossil fuel industry was subsidized in 2022. That's $5.9 trillion a year.[42]

---

41 Whitehouse.gov, "The Long-Term Strategies of the United States: Pathways to Net-Zero Greenhouse Gas Emissions by 2050," Whitehouse, November 2021, accessed April 8, 2022, https://www.whitehouse.gov/wp-content/uploads/2021/10/US-Long-Term-Strategy.pdf.

42 Lee Camp, "Fossil Fuels Subsidized at Rate of $11 Million per Minute," MR Online, October 3, 2022, accessed December 20, 2022, https://mronline.org/2022/10/03/fossil-fuels-subsidized-at-rate-of-11-million-per-minute/.

BASIC ECONOMICS: SUPPLY AND DEMAND

Because fossil fuels are nonrenewable and their source is limited, they will increasingly be harder (and more expensive) to obtain. Less supply will mean higher prices.

Carbon-neutral energy sources are becoming more widely available, but they often aren't yet as cost competitive as their fossil fuel counterparts, at least not to the average person paying the bill. But what you see on your monthly utility bill doesn't even accurately reflect the cost of producing and supplying energy to your home or business. Fossil fuels are still heavily subsidized by tax dollars in ways that renewable energy sources are not. If renewable energy sources were being subsidized to the same extent as fossil fuels, they would be the same cost to consumers (if not cheaper).[43] The executive order to bring the electricity industry to net-zero emissions by 2035 suggests that a shift is coming in this regard.

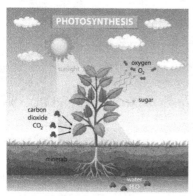

Plants Are Awesome[44]

However, reducing carbon dioxide emissions is not going to be enough. There's already too much carbon dioxide in the atmosphere. We need to start pulling carbon dioxide out of the atmosphere as well, and it needs to happen fast. There are a variety of approaches to achieving drawdown of atmospheric carbon dioxide. News

---

43 "Majority of New Renewables Undercut Cheapest Fossil fuel on Cost," IRENA, June 22, 2021, accessed December 20, 2022, https://www.irena.org/news/pressreleases/2021/Jun/Majority-of-New-Renewables-Undercut-Cheapest-Fossil-Fuel-on-Cost.

44 Brgfx, "Photosynthesis in Plants," Freepik, retrieved May 5, 2023, from https://www.freepik.com/free-photos-vectors/photosynthesis.

trends focus on technological innovations. Many of these seem as if they could work; however, at this point their efficacy is unproven, and their development will likely be expensive and cost-prohibitive, especially when thinking of deploying them on a scale massive enough to make a difference. At least for now, these cannot be the focus of our solution— sorry, Star Trek fans. Fortunately, right now, we can use nature's time-tested technology: plants. Plants work their magic to sequester carbon dioxide from the atmosphere and put it back into the soil.

MY FAVORITE STAR TREK GADGETS

- Warp Drive (obviously): You get to go fast
- Hypospray: A shot without the shot, medicine goes through the skin without the prick
- Universal Translators: I guess smart phones can kind of do this now (Tablets also appeared on Star Trek long before they were mainstream)
- Tricorder: Scan and analyze basically anything about an environment
- Replicators: What started as one glass of wine can become a party
- Transporter beam: Zaps you into sparkly dust and deposits you anywhere you want to go with a homing device when locked on to "your signature"
- Communicators: Otherwise known as today's cell phones

The National Public Utility Council

A few years ago, I was invited to sit on a panel to discuss the topic of decarbonization efforts for utilities (a Tier 2: CEO Environmental Powerhouse engagement). I didn't honestly know what I was doing there. The other panelists were representatives from large utilities. I had worked with utilities for a long time, but not on decarbonization, and I wasn't exactly sure how I was supposed to contribute to the panel.

The panelists were talking about the struggles utilities face in enacting decarbonization efforts. At some point, the representative from a utility in Arizona presented an issue her company was having around decarbonization regulation in sovereign nations. (Arizona includes a substantial portion of native land managed by tribal nations to which utility companies can provide power, but the laws that govern how this is done on those nations are tribal rather than federal.) She asked if anyone else on the panel had dealt with similar issues; if so, how they've handled it or could anyone suggest possible solutions.

The representative from a utility in Texas told her about a massive solar project that he had been involved in that had similar sensitive community interaction. His project wasn't based in a sovereign nation but had some similar complications and had been quite successful. The representative from the utility in Arizona got a great deal out of the advice.

"Do you guys get together and talk about what's working and what's not working like this?" I asked. "Do you share lessons learned, ideas, solutions?" It obviously seemed beneficial.

"No, we don't," the other panelists answered.

"Why not?" I asked, which seems to be my most asked questions.

Utilities are basically regional monopolies and not in competition with one another, so there was no reason for them not to share information.

Their response was basically: "We'll never do it. We've got too many other fish to fry." They didn't have the time, or couldn't make the time, and didn't have a foundation for organizing such an endeavor or the people to organize it.

But there were other reasons that nationwide utilities were not in conversation with one another. Utilities are large, bureaucratic organizations that are solely focused on their own communities— their grid and the customers they serve. They don't think outside of their own region or company. In many ways this makes sense. They each operate in unique geographical areas that have location-specific climate-related, social, and other concerns—the challenges of supplying energy in low-income Arizona deserts are different from those of the high-income high mountains in Colorado or retirement communities on the beaches of Florida. They are also a somewhat archaic industry that would never invest in an effort that doesn't directly and immediately contribute to their own company, unless they were required to.

"Wouldn't it be helpful to be in communication?" I asked.

"Yes," everyone said, but no one volunteered to organize. It wasn't going to happen.

HOW TO MAKE THINGS HAPPEN

It takes some effort to make things happen. Here's how we make things happen in my companies Motive Power and 10/6 Professional Services and with our efforts through the Gulch Foundation.

Organization: People want to just show up. They need clear instructions and scheduled meetings.

Deadlines: Without due dates, no one turns in their homework.

Incentives: Smiley face stickers (in all their forms) go a long way to encourage participation and action.

Put one foot in front of the other and keep going. Sooner or later you have something to work with.

"If I set up a scenario where we could communicate like this on a more regular basis, would you participate?" I asked.

"Yes," many of them said.

HOW TO MAKE THINGS HAPPEN II

There are various ways to get folks interested in projects and actions, but my favorite by far is peer pressure. As soon as someone sees that someone else whom they admire is involved, they are hooked.

The National Public Unity Council (NPUC) was born. The NPUC is comprised of big and small utilities from all over the country. Representatives from these utilities meet every other month in a roundtable format (virtual at first, due to COVID) to discuss the barriers to decarbonization and the ways that different utilities have met those challenges. The members represent forty of the fifty states. They come from different backgrounds and political perspectives, represent a range of socioeconomic and geographic populations, and have a range of ways in which they generate energy.

This year the NPUC together identified five major factors that are slowing decarbonization efforts by utilities:

1. **Utilities Need New and Innovative Technology** that can generate greener power and is reliable and safe. Much has already been developed, but not enough. It takes about ten years for utilities to put new technology into use because of federal and state regulations. (There are bigger ramifications to accepting and adopting new technology in the utility sector than in other sectors; it has to work well and work the first time. The consequences of failure are dramatic: When the power goes out, people die in hospitals.)

THE SAME CONVERSATION AGAIN

I noticed I was having some of the same conversations with utilities that I was having with farmers. They had apprehension about adopting new technologies and ways of doing things. Substantial risk was involved. In both cases I heard variations of:

"This seems complicated/difficult."

"What if it doesn't work?"

I find that folks are only interested in trying something new under two circumstances:

1. When they see an advantage to themselves, or

2. They have no other options.

In terms of climate change, we are working with both.

2. **Utilities Need to Educate the Populace** on new methods of providing energy so that their customer base is receptive to innovative ideas. If the utility says, "I'm going to start running hydrogen into your house because it's greener," the general populace, myself included, will say, "Wait a minute. Is that safe? And by the way, how do I cook an egg with hydrogen?" The utilities need ways to increase awareness and understanding both about the economic and social costs of the current way to doing things and the greener solutions to help consumers embrace change.

3. **Utilities Need Funding**, because everything costs money. Right now each utility is responsible for organizing and paying for infrastructure themselves. In order to optimize grids across the whole country, this infrastructure needs to be expanded and connected. Working together on a project of this scale is

not necessarily in the purview of the utilities. This really needs to be a federally funded initiative; it is a federal-level problem.

WE DID IT BEFORE; WE CAN DO IT AGAIN

During FDR's New Deal, the Works Progress Administration hired crews to build the interstate highways that we still use today. It was a well-funded program. And because it was federal, designers were thinking about the nation as a whole when configuring the system, which means we can all get our kicks on Route 66.

4. **Utilities Need Unique Solutions** that incorporate other industries to create economic options for large diverse communities. Utilities face unique situations with specialized socioeconomic and environmental challenges. In other words, they are all dealing with their own stuff. Different locations mean drastically different environmental challenges but also dramatically different socioeconomic populations. A utility in rural Alabama may serve a consumer with a median household income of $30,000, whereas a utility in San Francisco may serve a population with a median household income of $400,000. Also drastically different options for energy sources—solar and wind potential—are regionally different.

5. Lastly, **Utilities Need Workforce Development.** Even if the utilities came up with fantastic solutions to easily, safely, and readily supply green energy, they have no one to deploy or maintain the new technology. They do not have a large enough emergent workforce, and the existing workforce is not yet trained in green energy technology.

Organizing the NPUC was a Tier 3 effort. I'm proud of the NPUC. It illustrates the power of collaboration and enterprise in developing business-led solutions, as well as the role of utilities in advancing decarbonization. The NPUC is working to bring significant change how energy in the US is produced, as well as to increase consumer awareness around green energy.

GET RICH WITHOUT TRYING

Through the NPUC, I connected utilities to one another and also placed Motive Power in an advisory, marketing, and research position at the center of that network. The mission of the NPUC is to help utilities accelerate their efforts to decarbonize, making impactful change at a societal level, but it also established Motive Power as an ESG thought leader in the utilities space.

From a business perspective, forming the NPUC turned out to be accidental genius (AG). Focusing on utilities seemed like an obvious thing, and that's why I overlooked its genius at the time. I work in consulting: project management, change, adoption, organizational development. What I was able to do through the NPUC venue was to marshal the direct attention of the utilities of the US as one person with one message. I now have a wide-open field for sales. I have not capitalized on this field, and I don't know that I will, but from an entrepreneurial standpoint, this is a bona fide miracle. People spend hundreds of thousands of dollars to prepare and go to conferences to achieve something close to this. And I did it on accident—AG. I had the right focus at the right moment and the right approach. Through trying to bring the utilities together, I gained direct access to an A-list of clients.

ESG actions are often good for business in surprising ways.

The initial vision and function of the NPUC was to help utilities work together on holistic and practical solutions to reach net-zero carbon dioxide emissions for all utilities across the nation, and that is working.

Now that the ending pandemic allows us to meet in person, we can take it even further; we are going to get fancy and create events where utilities can showcase the strategies that they have implemented successfully. It will be a show-and-tell of innovation where utilities can receive individual and institutional recognition from peers. Hopefully these events will also use some competitive spirit to encourage companies to implement new strategies. Our first showcase took place in Sacramento where we hosted representatives from utilities from all over the nation who had the opportunity to explain the approaches and strategies they have in use and those that they intend to implement in the future. There was also a closed forum where representatives from utility organizations could discuss what was going on in their utility. Of course, we also had an open bar to ensure that it's a party (another way to encourage participation in these optional educational opportunities).

NPUC EVENT COCKTAILS

- Electric Lemonade
- The Transmitter
- Undergrounder
- Workforce Development
- Vodka Kilowatt
- The Decarbonizer
- Net-Zero (nonalcoholic)

Decarbonizaation Report

Shortly after I began writing this book, the NPUC, along with Motive Power and Visual Capitalist, distributed the first Annual Utility Decarbonization Report—a project that was a year in the making.

The report was publicly available on September 19, 2022, a date I chose because it's National Talk-Like-A-Pirate Day —a holiday that just doesn't get enough attention. It also turns out to be the start of climate week in New York—that was a happy accident, although it looked like brilliant planning.

MY FAVORITE PIRATE FACTS

The eye patch is part of the standard pirate costume, but this was actually a common item for sailors (or at least captains of ships) in general. Wearing a patch over one eye was a trick to help see in the dark below deck. The idea being that the covered eye was already adjusted to darkness.

The famous pirate Blackbeard intimidated captives and his ranks by tying hemp to his beard and setting it on fire.

Pirate ships worked on a democratic system with voting used to make group decisions, like to where the ship should navigate and how stolen loot should be divided. Each pirate ship had its own rules and code that had to be agreed to by all those on board.

There were great women pirates.[45]

Within the Decarbonization Report is an index that ranks the thirty largest investor-owned utilities in the US according to their decarbonization goals and their emissions output. We chose to focus on those utilities because they have the largest reach in terms of the customers or areas they serve and therefore could feasibly have a wider footprint and a taller challenge when it comes to getting to net-zero.

---

45   Nassau Paradise Island, "ARRR, Did You Know? 10 Fun Pirate Facts and Myths," Nassau Paradise Island, June 4, 2014, https://www.nassauparadiseisland.com/members/portal/arrr-did-you-know-10-fun-pirate-facts-and-myths.

The report showcases utilities who are striving for and making clean energy a priority for their organizations and our country. The report is focused largely on best in class—who's killing it and who's not. Surprisingly the top five are geographically dispersed (not only in California and other areas where representatives and others have for many years spoken to environmental concerns).

The report also works to demystify the utility industry. I've been paying an electric bill for decades, and before starting the NPUC, I didn't understand half the acronyms itemized on the bill. I paid; the lights stayed on in the house—it was basically magic. Along with some basic clarification about how utilities operate, the report addresses the five barriers to decarbonization and works to educate the public about the challenges that utilities face in trying to provide climate-friendly solutions. Utilities' contribution to carbon dioxide emissions are not all their fault, and certainly not an issue they can remedy by themselves. They need a consortium of groups and services to assist them on their race to net-zero emissions.

This report will likely be the first of many that I do looking at other industries, but I chose to focus this Decarbonization Report on the public utilities sector because I've worked with utilities for many years, I know the industry well, and I'm good at working with utilities. Also human reliance on power (electricity and gas) is on the rise as we move toward automation. Right now utilities and transportation account for 75 percent of greenhouse gas emissions across the world,[46] meaning this is where I can have the biggest impact.

The intent of the report is to reach investors. Most of the world's largest investors are invested in energy because it's safe and exponentially growing, but most investors are also aware of the ecological

---

46 Hannah Ritchie, "Sector by Sector: Where Do Global Greenhouse Gas Emissions Come from?" Our World in Data, September 18, 2020, accessed April 8, 2022, https://ourworldindata.org/ghg-emissions-by-sector.

economy and the shift toward ESG—which means that ecologically oriented companies are going to make more money in the future.

I say "most" investors because there are a few holdouts. In conducting research for the Decarboniza-tion Report, I learned that Berkshire Hathaway, run by Warren Buffet, is the largest investor in utilities across the US and that Warren Buffett

READING FOR EXTRA CREDIT

The Annual Decarbonization Report:

doesn't believe in the future of ESG or related investments.[47] This is likely because he's ninety years old and has gotten this far in life without having to view the world through an ecological economy lens, but we really do need to get Warren Buffet, and other big investors like him, on board.

Bill Gates, on the other hand, is savvy about green energy tech-nology. Now that the Decarbonization Report has been published, I intend to talk to Bill and see if he has talked to Warren. The way to influence business is to follow the money.

Mostly the Decarbonization Report gives information to the people who can truly influence the space: investors. If Bill Gates, or an investor like him, finds in the Decarbonization Report that an energy company in which he invests is failing to meet decarbonization goals, he can demand change in exchange for his continued investment.

In this way we can enable financial incentives to shift the ways that energy is produced rather than relying on changes in energy policy.

---

47 Simon Moore, "Buffett Shares His Unconventional Views on ESG Investing," Forbes, May 3, 2021, accessed December 20, 2022, https://www.forbes.com/sites/simonmoore/2021/05/02/buffett-shares-his-unconventional-views-on-esg-investing/.

WHEN THIS BOOK BECOMES A MOVIE

INT. WARREN BUFFET OFFICE (DAY)

Anthony Michael Hall playing BILL GATES walks into WARREN BUFFETT'S office

GATES: I noticed that you are an investor-owned company and that you don't spend any money on decarbonization efforts. (beat) I'm your largest investor. If you would like my five billion dollars next year, I'd like to see you rearrange your portfolio.

BUFFET: I am a huge fan of fossil fuels. I feel like they are my people, and I am soon to join them.

The Cow Jumped Over The Moon

I am confident that if we, being humanity, work together and work hard, we can achieve drawdown. I realize those are big ifs to expect from the entire population of the world, but the formation and achievements of the NPUC in only a few short years give me hope. The human race is creative and intelligent enough to develop and embrace clean energy technologies and to change the way we produce and even use energy—in all its forms.

Here's an inspiring story. When I was younger, I worked for many years on ranches in Northern California. What I learned about cows is that they can jump, and they're kind of indestructible. Far too often these unbelievable, horrible human beings would drive by the ranch and shoot my cattle—for fun, as though they had not discovered things like hobbies, pool parties, and sex. Once one of my cows got her neck blown out, and she was still sitting there grazing because she hadn't bled out yet. Obviously we had to put her down, but it was amazing to see this cow with this hole in her neck just eating, because that was what she knew how to do.

All those phrases you heard when you were a kid about cows are true. Cows can't jump over the moon, but they can definitely jump. And the reason the "cows come home" is because the cows left. Cows are always getting into trouble. One night I got called because my Angus bull had jumped the fence. He was black, so not easily visible in the dark of a rural roadway at night, and had made his way to the road where he got plowed into by a Cadillac. It wasn't good, for the bull or the Cadillac.

A QUOTE FROM FAMOUS ANTHROPOLOGIST, MARGARET MEAD *(VIA DR. TATIANA)*

"Never doubt that a small group of thoughtful, committed citizens can change the world; indeed, it's the only thing that ever has."[48]

This bull was in trouble. He was hobbling around and likely had a broken back leg. The Cadillac was totaled, but the driver was okay. I needed to get the bull back into the fence, which was a huge task, quite literally, given the weight and size of the bull. There was no way that I could move him without large machinery. He needed to move himself. I chased, lured, and tempted him back through the fence.

While I was dealing with the police and the Cadillac driver, the bull hobbled down to a little creek that ran through the property. I figured I would put him down in the morning. The next day I went to check on him, and remarkably he seemed to be doing okay. He was drinking water and didn't have a fever to indicate an infection. He was lying down, and in pain, but getting better. I figured I'd keep an eye on him for a few days and put him down if his condition degraded.

---

48 Nancy Lutkehaus, *Margaret Mead: The Making of an American Icon*, (2008: Princeton University Press), 261.

PUT OUT TO PASTURE

When animals are terminally ill on a ranch or farm, they aren't always brought to the vet to nurse them back to health from catastrophic injuries like the pet cat who slept on your head for sixteen years. There is no music, no essential oils, no pillows, no petting. There is euthanasia (or a shotgun), and if you are so inclined, a prayer.

I'll be damned if two weeks later that bull didn't get himself up. He had some motivation. He saw his cows in the other pasture, got to his feet, walked up the hill, went straight through a barbed-wire fence, (because fences are only suggestions to bulls), and mounted one of the cows. If he could do that, I figured he was fine.

There's a metaphor in here: the earth isn't shot in the head and waiting to bleed out while we munch on grass with no hope of recovery; we're merely maimed by the Cadillac of carbon dioxide emissions. But no one can move us toward change, we have to get up and get back in the field on our own. Given our creativity and intelligence, we are able solve the problem of climate change. What we really need is the proper motivation. If an attractive cow on a high hill isn't motivating for you, imagine better weather, business opportunity, and a healthier life.

Take Action: Get Organized

Revel in this possibility of drawdown. It can happen. We need to be educated about the problem, open to a wide suite of solutions, and willing to work together. Here are some ways that you can learn about and educate others about the specific causes of carbon dioxide emissions, possible solutions, and a path to organizing and implementing these solutions in a larger community.

Tier 1: The Savvy At-Home Composter

1. Educate yourself about drawdown (websites, films, articles, etc.) and on all the industries that can positively enact drawdown: everything from bicycles to buildings. Drawdown is real and reachable: https://drawdown.org/.

2. Grow things. ANYONE can grow things, no matter where they live or how they live: plant a garden, put a pot in your window. EVERY SINGLE PLANT COUNTS. If there is absolutely no space where you live, look into community gardening or parks, or …

3. Start a community garden, initiate a local park restoration, volunteer for efforts to greenify areas, or contribute to local outdoor shared spaces.

4. Talk to your family and friends about what you are doing and what you have learned.

Tier 2: The CEO Environmental Powerhouse

1. Utilize your philanthropic sensibilities toward projects that enact drawdown (education and action).

2. Also take the Tier 1 Savvy At-Home Composter actions.

Tier 3: The Big Cheese World Changer

1. Participate in COP seminars.

2. Engage and educate world leaders on drawdown.

3. Work with regulators and governments to define standards and reporting governance in government and in industry. Define your competitive advantage. Once ESG governance is compulsory (coming soon to a theater near you), being ahead of the knowledge curve will give a leg up to those who have not accounted for it.

4. Work with your teams to model profitable ways to enact drawdown within industry.
5. Invest in farmland and farming institutions that have an eye toward drawdown.
6. Participate in legislation to:
    a. Revolutionize the energy industry with your investment dollars.
    b. Reconfigure the cement industry with your investment dollars.
    c. Recast the transportation industry (already in motion with movement to EV) with your investment dollars.
7. Also take the Tier 2: CEO Environmental Powerhouse actions.
8. Also take the Tier 1: Savvy At-Home Composter actions.

PART 2

Triple Win

CHAPTER 6

Green Is Green

Farm Day 1

When I decided to take the Tier 3: Big Cheese World Changer action and start the Gulch Environmental Foundation, I was midlife processing (not in crisis). I decided I wanted to spend more time doing what I liked to do. What I like to do is: 1) grow things, and I'm good at that, and 2) throw parties, and I'm really good at that. So the Gulch Environmental Foundation was born; its main project became Rainmaker Farm.

Once the farm was underway, and I had put some stuff in the ground, it was time for the party—well, not exactly a party. I decided to take a Tier 2: CEO Environmental Powerhouse action and invite my employees from Motive Power and 10/6 Professional Services to have a company retreat on the farm and plant trees. We were going to have fun but also work our asses off.

It was February. In Oklahoma. Sixty-seven employees were on their way.

DETAILS OF THE PREPARATION FOR BUDDING PARTY PLANNERS

A great deal of preparation had gone into the retreat. I had:

- Booked hotels and flights for everyone, as well as busses to and from the farm.
- Ordered rock star port-a-potties. The only structure on the farm at that

time was what I call "the tiny house," an eight-by-sixteen-foot gorgeous structure that, at that time, had electricity but no plumbing.

- Met with vendors, including the nicest steakhouse in Oklahoma City, to organize catering.
- And, of course, stocked up on snacks, wine, and other essentials.

This was all in addition to getting things prepared for the actual planting.

Rural Oklahoma may seem like an unusual company retreat. Motive Power's other retreat is an annual trip to Cabo, Mexico, where we stay at a five-star resort for four days. There are meetings but also the beach, and employees are allowed to bring spouses. It's a gorgeous event. Planting trees on a farm is a different experience, but I believe a valuable one and more than a triple win: 1) It got my employees interested in Rainmaker Farm; 2) it gave me an opportunity to force some environmental education on my employees by making the film *Kiss the Ground* mandatory viewing before the trip; 3) through hands-on work during the trip, my employees developed a comprehensive level of understanding about ecology and a deeper appreciation for the ethos of my companies (sustainability, ESG, and making a real impact); and 4) the communal experience did the things that all retreats are supposed to do—built community and solidified company culture. I would argue that working hard at the farm had greater impacts on employees than lounging on the beach in Cabo.

We were going to plant perimeter trees, which are controversial in

DO THIS NOW! *RIGHT NOW!*

Seriously? What are you, in third grade? This was assigned in Part 1 of the book. You are behind. Get it together. Go watch *Kiss the Ground*. It's got high production value. There are real celebrities in it. It's worth your time.

A NOTE FROM DR. TATIANA

Farmers and the ecologists at OSU taught me that this part of Oklahoma is known as the cross timbers, which is an area of transition from the forests in the east to the prairies in the west.

A NOTE FROM DR. TATIANA
(TO RAIN ON MY PARADE)

For the record, the best plants for sequestering carbon are actually deep-rooted native grasses, although trees are also very beneficial.

BANNED

Due to their release of allergy-causing pollens, mulberry trees have been banned in several southwestern cities including El Paso, Tucson, Las Vegas, and Albuquerque.[49]

Oklahoma. Nobody in Oklahoma likes trees. I had various people tell me, "These are the plains states, trees don't grow here," which is bullshit and in no way discouraged me. Trees are always more than a triple win: 1) windbreak, 2) shade, 3) topography, and 4) carbon dioxide sequestration. I wanted to plant trees because planting things is the best way to sequester carbon dioxide, which is Rainmaker Farm's purpose.

Before the retreat, the trees that I'd ordered (minus the mulberry trees) had been delivered via semi truck. They were huge; twelve-feet tall with root balls too large to wrap my arms around. The holes had been dug by machines, and the trees set in. The mission of the retreat was to remove the canvas wrap from the roots, stake the trees north to south (against the wind), and fill the holes with dirt. It sounds simple, but it was a difficult task.

49 D. Prokop, "3 Decades into El Paso's Ban on New Mulberries, Existing Trees Are Nearing End of Life," El Paso Matters, July 7, 2022, https://elpasomatters.org/2021/11/29/3-decades-into-el-pasos-ban-on-new-mulberries-existing-trees-are-nearing-end-of-life/.

The day before the retreat, I was ready for the troops, and then calamity struck.

When I arrived in Oklahoma three days before the retreat, the farmers from the local community who were helping me were pessimistic about the weather. I didn't listen to them because it was 85°F, and farmers spend 90 percent of their life talking about the weather, and their outlook is usually negative. I wasn't buying what I thought was their hysteria.

SOME ADVICE ABOUT WORKING RETREATS: GO FOR 100 PERCENT PARTICIPATION

When I put together retreats like this, I make sure there is something to do for every physical type. Someone might have an injury, or not be physically fit, or extremely tall, or short, or large, or small. I make sure there's always a job for everybody. I want 100 percent participation.

Once I was doing a river cleanup with my employees, and there were some young men in their early twenties—athletic specimens. They had a lot of energy, and they needed a lot to do. I asked them to dig out these tires from the river—I don't know if you've ever tried to dig out a heavy tire from the soft, cement-like silt at the bottom of the river, but it is near impossible. But these young men took on the challenge. An hour and three broken shovels later, they yelled together, "Victory." It was the right physical task for them.

On the day of the retreat, the entire country was sunny with blue skies. Except for Oklahoma City. A meteorological map showed an entirely clear North American continent, with a single red spiral of death directly over Rainmaker Farm. In Oklahoma City, the coldest day in recent history had kicked off an ice storm.

All flights to Oklahoma City were canceled. Most of my employees were stuck in airports. "If you can't make it to Oklahoma City," I texted out, "you know what to do."

"Hit the bar," the texts came back.

And the texts kept on coming with ideas about how to get to the farm, reports on local airports, updates on the weather, selfies with new friends stuck in similar situations. We were apart but still on an epic team-building adventure. Fourteen brave souls made it to the farm, including Dr. Tatiana.

Our first day of planting was a blustery 20°F (5°F with windchill) and snowy, but not unbearable (especially for me and my two employees from Minnesota). We had a heater in the little house, cocoa on tap, catering for sixty-seven people, and 144 trees to plant. We went out into the cold and got it done. Even the girly girls were out there digging in the frozen-solid soil. There was a real feeling that we were embarking on something as a team that was bigger than any one of us. People wanted to be involved. They were driven not only to be included but also to include themselves and to do good things. We got twenty trees planted. I was very proud. We continued to text out our big adventure to those who couldn't make it.

You might ask, how can you consider that retreat a success rather than a failure? How was that good for my business? The answer is that the Rainmaker Farm retreat, even with only fourteen employees in attendance, was a huge, long-term financial success. The retreat cost me about $30,000, which was nothing compared to my return on investment in terms of internal and external marketing.

THE GOLD STAR GOES TO

Two of my employees from Minnesota who drove eleven hours to Rainmaker Farm.

HONORARY MENTION GOES TO

Two others from Los Angeles who drove to alternative airports to catch flights that arrived to Oklahoma City just before the airport shut down.

A LITTLE MORE ABOUT INTERNAL MARKETING

As with many other companies, Motive Power and 10/6 Professional Services lost some ground in terms of company culture during the COVID shutdown when everyone was working remotely. But also COVID generally shifted people away from work. This isn't entirely bad. Before COVID, many people were over engaged with work, work was the end all and be all, and people's life goals had to do with climbing the ladder. COVID shifted priorities but, like a pendulum, overcorrected to create another unhealthy relationship with work. Now employees report that they can't come into work or can't finish a project because they're waiting for the washing machine repair guy or going to a kid's piano recital. These were all issues that they negotiated with work before COVID, but now these personal issues take precedence. Showing up to plant trees is an exactly opposite behavior. It requires you to prioritize work appropriately, set goals, work hard, and you are rewarded with an immediate sense of accomplishment for that work.

And teams bond over achieving a task. It doesn't have to be an insurmountable task, although the more heroic the task, the more bonding occurs. The task has a larger impact when it has a physical element rather than only a cerebral element. Some of my teams build software, which is very cerebral. Those teams bond, and their working relationships develop when they have come in over the weekend, eat bad pizza, and physically be together to work. Accomplishing tasks together is what creates teams that are actual teams rather than a group of people who are together. Businesses benefit from having teams that work well together: They are more efficient, good at solving problems, and generally better performing. Planting trees on the farm checks the basic boxes of team building and solidifying company culture.

The employees who came to Rainmaker Farm on that first trip, and the trip that followed in April, also became invested in the company and the company's ethos in a way that they never could have simply by working in the office or even being treated to a working vacation in Cabo. Weeks and months after the trips, employees were asking me how the trees were doing, asking for pictures. Parents told their kids about the experience, and kids became interested in what their parents were doing at work. People told me stories about watching *Kiss the Ground* with their families. Employees were bragging to their friends about all the good work they were doing. They were proud, involved, and energized by the experience. The financial advantage of the retreat can be calculated as follows: retaining employees versus replacing and training new people, increased and improved production from engaged and invested employees, and the efficiency of employees working well together toward a common goal. In terms of Motive Power and 10/6 Professional Service's goals to move industry toward sustainability, the experience of planting trees at Rainmaker Farm made believers of those who thought the task was impossible. The project is surprisingly and strangely hopeful. It is not the doom-and-gloom conversation that people are used to having about the environment.

MY AIRPORT CONVERSATION DURING A DIFFERENT TRIP TO RAINMAKER FARM

On the way home from Oklahoma City once, months before the company retreat, I was at the Delta counter switching my seat, and the Delta agent asked, "What are you doing here in Oklahoma?"

"We just planted our first wheat harvest," I told her. Then I told her about buying the farm and my mission to demonstrate the benefits of regenerative farming.

"I'm gonna cry," she said. "Can I come over and hug you?"

She walked around the desk and gave me a hug.

A Little Education: A Brief Lesson in the History of the Economy

As the economy shifts, the relationship between employees and their employer companies also shift. In the sixties, seventies, and eighties, the economy was functional. If you were an engineer, you often stayed an engineer for the duration of your career (starting as a junior engineer, promoted to senior engineer, principal engineer, etc.). You worked for one or maybe two companies in your lifetime and focused on being an engineer for that company.

EXAMPLE: FRENCH FRY ENGINEER

Let's, for example, say that you were a french fry engineer (because everyone likes fries) for a fast-food franchise. As an engineer you might develop different french fry formulas, develop machinery that produced fries faster, etc.

The nineties and two-thousands added a projectized thrust to this economy. The company structure for employees became more matrixed and less linear. Employees were assigned to projects where they might conduct multiple tasks. As an engineer, you no longer moved through the ranks in the same way you did in the sixties, but from one project to the next. You may work for multiple companies in your lifetime, moving on after a project is completed.

Now the work environment is shifting again. Engineers still work on projects and for

EXAMPLE: FRENCH FRY ENGINEER 2

The fry engineer for the fast-food franchise might be assigned to work the Seasoned Fry Project, or the Fat-Free Fry Project. The focus of the projects was still functional, but each employee was centered around different projects.

EXAMPLE:
FRENCH FRY ENGINEER 3

As a french fry engineer, you still work on fry projects (curly, crinkled, bite-size); however, now those projects need to include an explanation to the rest of the business world, the fry industry, and the customer base, on how the new fry product line is ecologically sustainable, affordable for low-income communities, and produced in ways that are fair to employees working for the company.

different companies as they did before, but now every project that they work on will in some way have an ESG focus. As with the previous phases, companies that ignore this trend will not survive. We are moving into an ESG and ecological economy.

Globally, nearly all (92 percent) of companies are adopting business strategies to become more sustainable and planning to increase their investment in sustainability initiatives to improve their ESG performances.[50] Eighty percent of leading companies around the world self-report on sustainability,[51] and 75 percent of Silicon Valley companies have a CSO (Chief Sustainability Officer).[52] In 2022 49 percent of organizations in the US had DEI (diversity, equity, and inclusion) programs;[53] 79 percent of those companies raised their budgets. That's a big deal. It means there is

50 Motive Power, "Ecological Economy," accessed August 24, 2023, https://www.motive-power.com/ecological-economy/.

51 Sean McCabe, "KPMG study: 80% of top companies now report on sustainability," Accounting Today, December 1, 2020, https://www.accountingtoday.com/news/eighty-percent-of-top-companies-now-report-on-sustainability-kpmg-study.

52 Motive Power, "Ecological Economy," accessed August 24, 2023, https://www.motive-power.com/ecological-economy/.

53 John Corrigan, "Only 34 & of companies have enough resources to support DEI initiatives," HRD, February 28, 2022, https://www.hcamag.com/us/specialization/corporate-wellness/only-34-of-companies-have-enough-resources-to-support-dei-initiatives/326842.

a social movement and an attempt at social understanding. Capitalism and business do not have reputations for being socially responsible enterprises, but they are also not stupid. They recognize that acting with an ESG lens is necessary moving forward.

DEFINED

I like to start with definitions of things. Here are some summaries from Merriam-Webster.

Ecological: Relating to or concerned with the relation of living organisms to one another and to their physical surroundings.[54] (Wow, that applies to everything.)

Economy: Wealth of resources of a country or region, especially in terms of the production of and consumption of goods and services.[55] (What are goods and services if not ecological, right?)

We used to trade nuts and berries for shells and rocks. The economy has always been based in ecology. Going forward we will not be able to offer anything of value for money, unless it is directly tied to, uh, an ecological pursuit.

The bottom line is that in order to survive going forward, businesses must adapt to consumer demand, employee passions, supply chains, etc. Businesses that don't keep up are violating a fundamental law of business: that what doesn't grow dies. This principle doesn't only apply to financial management but also to perspective. Climate change has an impact on all aspects of business. Savvy businesses are viewing those impacts through a climate change lens and not only keeping up with these changes but on the forefront anticipating

---

54 Merriam-Webster.com Dictionary, s.v. "ecological," accessed May 23, 2023, https://www.merriam-webster.com/dictionary/ecological.

55 Merriam-Webster.com Dictionary, s.v. "economy," accessed May 23, 2023, https://www.merriam-webster.com/dictionary/economy.

COMPANIES THAT REFUSED TO INNOVATE

- Blackberry
- Kodak
- Blockbuster
- Commodore
- Atari
- MapQuest

change and developing an ecological and ESG mindset that will give their business an advantage.

There is limited opportunity to be on the forefront of this movement. I liken it to surfing a wave; the companies on the forefront are riding the wave, and they're adapting readily to the shifts in pace and angle. The companies that fail to adapt will wipe out, and those who have not managed to paddle in yet will miss the wave entirely. The chance to ride won't last forever. This is an ecological market window that will close, and companies who are not attentive to it will be shut out. ESG is the future.

HOW TO SURF

1. Find a wave

2. Paddle to match the momentum of the wave

3. Ride the wave by shifting your weight to stay balanced on the board

Okay, But How Do I Make Money Off This?

The goal of business is to make money. Companies are only willing to go green and follow ESG standards if they are economically sustainable or better yet profitable. This is no problem. There are some obvious ways that meeting ESG standards are immediately cost beneficial for companies.

1. Direct Savings: Motive Power recently worked on a project to identify attributes within a portfolio to determine what main-

tenance and repair work on various gas lines could be bundled together. Bundling these services is not only beneficial for the environment, but also they will cut costs for the company. Minimizing mobilization (less trips to a repair site) means less carbon dioxide emissions (ESG) and decreased overall spending on repairs ($), less shutdowns and customer complaints (PR), etc. Being efficient and not wasteful with resources is also financially beneficial.

2. Marketing Benefits: Companies, like Boody, make money by marketing to consumers concerned about the environment and social issues.

3. Increased Customer Base: Becoming ESG compliant not only keeps activists at bay, but it also attracts consumers. Other companies, like Ford, create product lines, like their electric truck, Lightning, that capitalize on the ESG-aware consumer.

4. Increased Investors: Becoming ESG compliant also attracts investors who want to align themselves with responsible companies who will succeed in the future as well as the present. These investors tend to be less fickle—people who invest in something because they believe in the cause are dedicated and more likely to stick with a company, even through difficult times.

5. Employee Retention: Businesses with an ESG mindset can attract and retain the best talent, meaning they have less attrition and less expenditures on hiring and training new people, and they have capable, motivated people working for them. Especially the younger generations joining the workforce want to work for impactful companies and want to make an impact through their work. Smart companies now hire people with that in mind—they intentionally shape their businesses' philosophies to be mission driven with an ESG-centered ethos that attracts smart, sophisticated employees.

Cheaters Never Win

At present, ESG compliance is self-reported. Reporting indicates an organization's focus on trying to achieve a greater good. In these reports companies can describe a company's vision, policies, practices, and the activities they embrace and undertake to support positive ESG efforts. The reports may include case studies, metrics, press coverage, and other information. Most of these reports are directed toward investors and shareholders, sometimes regulators, or as with my companies, presented to clients and the public.

ESG REPORTING IS CHANGING

The SEC and ISO are the first organizations to begin solidifying mandatory reporting and its applications, although there are various initiatives underway through private enterprise and governmental entities to make ESG reporting regulated, mandated, and mandatory (it is already mandatory in some countries). This reporting will support carbon tax credits and other business vehicles.

Consumers and industries are turning up the pressure on companies to reduce their environmental impacts and to engage in ESG reporting. Many companies understand that being green, or at least looking like they conform to ESG standards, can attract customers and employees and generally give them an advantage in the market. Because people are opportunists (and assholes), some of these companies represent themselves falsely in order to reap the benefits of going green without really taking measures to do so: Greenwashing.

ESG reporting is largely analyzed and policed by the community. Social media and other ways to easily access information bring a kind of transparency—consumers and other players in the industry and check up on your business and, in a fourth-grade fashion, tattle or give you gold stars. If your company is genuinely performing well and making an impact that benefits the world, people will notice, and word will spread. If your company is not engaged in ESG practices, or is claiming to be but not performing, that word will also spread. Greenwashing and false reporting will also soon face more serious scrutiny. The SEC is launching a Climate and ESG Task Force to focus on disclosure ESG-related misconduct.[56]

GREENWASHING: A DEFINITION

(From Motive Power's ESG Course)

Intentionally deceiving customers or investors into believing that your company is environmentally conscious when your actions do not support the claim.

Greenwashing also happens in less official ways wherein companies suggest they are green, often by using fluffy, meaningless jargon (eco-friendly), irrelevant imagery (landscape shots of random places at sunrise), or third-party endorsement akin to imaginary friends (Dr. So-and-So of some-clinic-they-hope-you-won't-look-up). They often use messages that misdirect, rather than lie outright, in order to tap into the ecological market without adopting a new mindset, developing a new product line, or making changes that have meaningful impacts.

ESG CERTIFICATION PROGRAMS

From the S&P 500 ESG Index

(Sidenote: this is the one Tesla got kicked out of because they didn't do well on the Social aspect of ESG.)

---

56   U.S. Securities and Exchange Comission, "Enforcement Task Force Focused on Climate and ESG Issues," accessed August 22, 2023, https://www.sec.gov/spotlight/enforcement-task-force-focused-climate-esg-issues.

GREEN SUGGESTIONS

My favorite examples are those ads for oil companies that show a beautiful long-haired child running through a field of wheat at sunset with a voiceover that talks about the sound of wind and joyful laughter and shows or mentions nothing that has anything to do with oil or petroleum on any level. The scenic images of nature suggest that the companies are stewards of the earth and disregard the fact that they are fossil fuel extractors.

Other companies cheat by making products that are good for the earth but are produced in ways that destroy the earth. Or emphasize one, tiny green attribute of their company while every other attribute of their production is nowhere near green.

Making it easier to bend the rules and warp the language is that there is not a central governance or guidance with specific parameters that define what ESG is or what it should be. It's a little like a class where the teacher lets you grade yourself. Companies come out with ESG reports based on what they've decided ESG should be, which is usually in line with whatever will make them look good. The SEC task force is also working on developing specific parameters for compliance with environmental issues and ESG standards. Change is coming.

A HYPOTHETICAL EXAMPLE

Energy-efficient light bulbs made in a factory that pollutes rivers.

Farm Day 2

In early April, months after our first company retreat to Rainmaker Farm, I gave the company retreat at Rainmaker Farm a second try. The neighboring farmers, who came to help during the first retreat, thought I was nuts, but they agreed to help again. I had more trees to plant, including smaller orchard trees. I also got roses and lavender to help feed the bees that were pollinating my farm and beehives (to hold those same bees) that needed to be assembled. This time the retreat was optional, and there was no ice storm. About thirty Motive Power and 10/6 Professional Services employees showed up ready to work.

I did my little "Hi, welcome to the farm" spiel and then started directing. "I need people planting trees; I need people planting bushes; I need people on layout; I need people on trash pickup." People broke into teams, rocked and rolled, and we had the whole orchard planted before lunch. Then we played cornhole. The power of manpower is amazing. Even the farmers were impressed. It was a great day.

A LITTLE MORE ABOUT EXTERNAL MARKETING

You can't beat word of mouth from genuinely enthused people.

The retreat gleaned tons of free PR. Employees reported telling friends and complete strangers about Rainmaker Farm, the retreat, and the ethos of Motive Power and 10/6 Professional Services. They talked about regenerative farming to their Uber drivers on the way to the airport, and when they were stuck in the airport, they told everyone at the bar about the project. And every story they told was connected to my companies.

The trip was a success. I got home, celebrated with copious amounts of champagne, and danced around my house, which I routinely do. Then I may or may not have drunk-texted some people a video that we'd made of our farm day.

One of the clients who I'd texted—the CEO of one of the largest food commodity brokers in the world—texted me back and said, "I want to organize a team-building activity for my employees at Rainmaker Farm. When can we come?"

It was another moment of accidental genius when I unintention-ally became a brilliant events planner for corporate team-building retreats. There's money in it for sure, if I want to go in that direction. The ways to make money from being green seem endless.

ANGEL'S DRUNK-DANCING BEACH HOUSE PLAYLIST

- Parliament
- Black-Eyed Peas
- Justin Timberlake
- Amy Winehouse
- Frank Sinatra
- Caro Emerald
- Lake Street Drive
- Michael Franti
- The Fugees
- Blonde
- Bob Marley
- James Brown

For now I am happy with all that Motive Power and 10/6 Professional Services accomplished during our two farm days at Rainmaker Farm. Physically we got a great deal done. Most importantly it got my employees invested in our company, our ethos, and the farm in remarkable ways. People are still messaging me and asking me in the hallways, "How are the trees?" and demanding that I send pictures.

The trips to Rainmaker Farm also connected my employees to a greater purpose. Planting trees, building bee boxes, and physically putting carbon back into the ground made people feel like they were saving the world. They felt like they did something tremendous. They felt that I, as their leader, had gifted them an opportunity they wouldn't otherwise have had. As an employer and someone with a mission, that level of motivation and emotional investment is invaluable.

Take Action: Join the Ecological Economy

My companies make money by being and having a reputation for being green. When I meet with current and prospective clients, I tell them about Rainmaker Farm. Recently I was talking with a medical device company about change management, project and portfolio optimization, and how they could get their products to market more effectively. We started with polite conversation.

"What did you do this weekend?" the reps asked.

BACKGROUND: MOTIVE POWER AND 10/6 PROFESSIONAL SERVICES

Two of my companies focus on capital project management and delivery, consultation, and related services. Motive Power does this through organizational development (process improvement, systems deployment, change adoption, change management, and data innovation) often using research conducted by the NPUC that offers a comprehensive and data-driven understanding of the utility industry as a whole. After Motive Power has delivered organizational change, or a system reporting, 10/6 Professional Services delivers based on what was achieved on the Motive Power platform. Motive Power might build a project control group and from that a project management group. Once those systems are in place, 10/6 continues to execute project management based on those systems.

"I was at the farm," I said.

"What were you doing at a farm?" they asked, and the conversation shifted from portfolio optimization to my progress with my latest wheat harvest. Rainmaker Farm is a tangible, hopeful project, and one that comes with pictures and videos of my employees happily freezing their butts off while planting trees. The way the client viewed me and Motive Power transitioned with the conversation. I was clearly genuine, able to take action, and creating solutions rather than dwelling on problems. Being a thought leader is what makes me money, and Rainmaker Farm displays my abilities.

Both Motive Power and 10/6 Professional Services also make money being green directly by supporting projects through the Gulch

Environmental Foundation and through our business by governing capital infrastructure projects through an ESG lens, aiding in change adoption, and offering innovative consulting that helps the companies we serve prepare to get on track and report their ESG progress. Meeting ESG standards, and making it known to the industry and larger communities that a company is ESG compliant, ultimately makes a company more successful—we help companies catch the wave and find the ride.

I have over twenty years of experience working with utilities, and I sometimes know the industry better than the people at the companies with whom I meet. On occasion I've gone to meet with a client after having read their annual report and said to them, "Did you know that you were supposed to be hitting ESG targets?" When they tell me they had no idea, I offer to help through consultation. "I heard that you're going up for VP next year. You're going to need to hit these targets. Let me help you get there." I explain how the company can get a handle on the situation and give them a plan to achieve the metric. "It will make your CEO look good. It will help your company make money. You'll get promoted. Everything will be great. And here's my bill." All I had to do was know about the ESG metric (something most people whom I meet with from the utility companies don't know), read their annual report, and have a plan to set and make goals. This is easy money, and you can similarly cash in.

THERE IS A WAY TO MONETIZE ANYTHING

Motive Power gets many benefits from our investment in the NPUC including connection to utilities (our current and potential clients), research that we can use to improve our consulting work (consulting in general is really all about information sharing), and free PR (it certainly ups your game if you're able to whip out something that your company has created on the subject matter or just share it with your clients so that they can use it). We can leverage the report to show that we are thought leaders in the utility industry, etc. But we could also directly monetize the NPUC:

We could charge an annual membership fee. In the way of other organizations (like the Electric Power Research Institute) where utilities would pay a membership fee on an annual basis to be invited into a more in-depth conversation.

We could sell the data that we have mined. We often receive data requests for deeper dives into specific areas, particular companies or a subset of companies, and we could easily compile this data and make it accessible (and marketable).

Establishing my companies as forward-thinking and cutting edge, through publications like the Decarbonization Report and other actions creates business opportunities and also means that we can start to raise prices and offer other products.

But most of all, this type of cutting-edge work leads to more high-value consulting. Clients seek our comprehensive expertise in ESG subject matter and its application to industries.

My companies, having invested in the research through the NPUC and designed the models for application, can piggyback off our in-house management consulting skillsets to provide better consulting to assess ESG positioning in industry, define tight goal sets, and chart a course to achieve them.

Tier 1: The Savvy At-Home Composter

1. Initiate a green movement at work or in your community as an educational outreach to those who participate. It:

    i. unites a community in a single effort,

    ii. helps the environment, and

    iii. becomes a visible, tangible action that is good for building a reputation (or PR).

COMPOSTING IN A CITY THAT PROMOTES COMPOSTING

Some cities and towns have adopted composting; it helps them manage their landfills better. If your city is one of these, ask for a "compost" can or something similarly named. It will come with guidance on what to compost and what not to. In addition to the city provided service, you will want a countertop compost capture can for when cooking or other household leftover stuff needs to be collected and then transported to the city compost can. This is a great job for kids.

COMPOSTING IN A RURAL AREA

This is the most optimal in my opinion—no smell, quick compost, and then easy transfer to your garden.

If you have the space to make your own compost pile here are the basics:

1. Along with all your kitchen scraps ensure you add fibrous things to it (leaves, lawn clippings, etc.)

2. Ensure you add some dirt

3. Moisture and heat content makes the compost go round

Tips:

- If your composts seems like dust, there is not enough water in it. Add water
- If you compost is growing things (seeded from your scraps or mold), it is not hot enough. Cover it and keep it in the sun

4. Turn the pile here and there

5. Add worms (believe it or not you can get these on Amazon)

Note: Compost sometime attracts nocturnal animals (racoon, skunk, whatever is in your area)

IN THE MIDDLE

If you are in an area with no room for a pile and no city services (although check, these are more available than you think), consider a compost bin. These are purchasable from Amazon or from your local Lowes, Home Depot, etc. Follow the instructions for composting. I find these work less well than the outdoor pile.

There are various books about composting available to get you started. "Let it Rot" is my favorite.

Tier 2: The CEO Environmental Powerhouse

1. Model environmentally conscious choices at work (informally educate). Make your passion visible to your employees. When your employees are committed to your company's ideals and working for things to which they subscribe, they will be better workers, your business will be more efficient, and you will make more money (and spend less money doing it). Sticky employees translate to intact cultures.

2. Formally educate your workforce. Chances are they have some knowledge on climate change, and chances are also that they don't have enough. More information will support any changes you may ask them to make going forward. You can do this with ESG or environmental courses, team-building exercises, reading and viewing requirements, etc.

3. Create an impact report for your organization.

4. Analyze your products or services to see how they align with ESG scorecards and implement regular reporting.

5. Align your companies' missions with aspects of ESG that resonate with you and your companies' products/services.

6. Consider joining the UN Corporate Sustainability Program: https://unglobalcompact.org/what-is-gc.

7. Market your ESG prowess for your business aims—increased revenues, increased evaluation, higher EBITA, more add backs, etc.

8. Also take the Tier 1: Savvy At-Home Composter actions.

Tier 3: The Big Cheese World Changer

1. Start an investment fund (similar to Al Gore's investment firm, Generation Investment Management) that is a standard fund, but one that utilizes investment strategies that are environmentally-centered. https://algore.com/project/generation-investment-management.

2. Start an organization (or several) that provides tools, training, and a strong network to enact change and promote drawdown.

3. Connect with Sir Ronald Cohen and reshape capitalism—after you read his book, *Impact*.

4. Also take the Tier 2: CEO Environmental Powerhouse actions.

5. Also take the Tier 1: Savvy At-Home Composter actions.

CHAPTER 7

Just Do It

Waiting for the Smart People

Climate change presents issues that seem too big for us as individuals, or even businesses, to handle: fires, floods, hurricanes, droughts, annual increases in global temperature, and the destruction, interruption of supply chains, and infrastructure failures that come with these natural disasters. Because the issues seem insurmountable, we tend to have this sense that the powers-that-be have it all under control. Surely *they* are keeping tabs on things. *They* won't allow anything apocalyptic to happen. We, the individuals and businesses, are waiting for *them*—the experts, the smart people, the authorities—to take control or advise us. But whatever powers-that-be that do exist are composed of everyday people like you and me. The experts are us. We are the smart people.

If you are waiting for the solution, I have good news: I have the solution. The bad news: You are the solution.

I frequently tell this to CEOs and other business leaders with whom I work. "Who gets things done?" I ask. "Entrepreneurs." Entrepreneurs don't wait for the government or other business leaders or other industries to hand us solutions. We are problem solvers willing to take action.

The first annual Decarbonization Report, published by the NPUC and Motive Power (a Tier 3 action), came out this spring (2023), and it's gorgeous. The intent of the report was to take research gathered by the NPUC related to the decarbonization efforts of utilities and move it into the marketing realm. The report defines and ranks utilities based on ESG measurements that we, the authors of the report, made up. The government is working on similar definitions and will likely come out with their own rankings eventually, and when they do so, we will adapt. In the meantime, we don't have time to wait. The Decarbonization Report is strategic and immediately necessary: It analyzes the top thirty investor-owned (meaning they must publish annual reports for investors that are publicly available) utilities and makes their annual reports and decarbonization efforts easily accessible to investors, or anyone, meaning that they are held accountable or rewarded for their actions. We didn't have time to wait for the government or some other organization of smart people to create the report. We are the smart people. We defined our metrics based on careful, in-depth analysis of the annual reports and other research; we know the industry; we are educated about the effects of various decarbonizing efforts.

Once we realize that there is no point in waiting for the smart people to come to our rescue, we need to overcome the other big obstacle that keeps us from taking action: fear of change. We do what we know, what is easy, and what we've been taught. People don't tend to break the status quo unless they have to. But entrepreneurs also excel on this front. We are adventurous and brave. Breaking the status quo is an adventure (and not one that will bankrupt you or ostracize you from your community).

I WAS TAUGHT TO DRIVE A FOSSIL FUEL CAR

I know how to change the oil, fill the tank, and get it serviced. Owning a fossil fuel car is familiar and comfortable, and so, without incentive, I am likely to choose to continue owning a fossil fuel car.

Building a Beehive

I had an issue at Rainmaker Farm. My farm needed some bees for pollination, so I started YouTubing and Googling the hell out of bees. The first thing I learned is that beekeepers typically work with bees by smoking them. Even if you hate honey (who hates honey?), it's necessary to harvest the honey periodically, or the bees will outgrow the hive. The traditional way to harvest honey is by blowing smoke at the hive, which makes the bees woozy and docile while the beekeeper pulls out the honeycomb frames, brushes the bees away, and drains the honey. It's invasive at least, and also a little like slipping the bees a mickey and robbing them blind. The process felt too gangster for a regenerative farm, so I kept up my internet research (with appropriate interruptions for videos about cute puppies, human anomalies you wouldn't believe, and incredible cake decoration).

FUN FACT

Bees are considered livestock.[57]

I learned about Flow Hives. Flow Hives allow you to collect honey without ever opening the hive. Flow Hives come with a prebuilt honeycomb surface that the bees build onto with wax and fill with honey. When you want to harvest the honey, you slide a lever that pulls the honeycomb structure apart, allowing the honey to flow out through a spout while the bees go about their business on the surface of the honeycomb. Then you shift it back into place. No bees get smoked; no bees get hurt; you don't even interrupt their conversations. Flow Hives seemed like the way to go.

---

57   Jim Belt, "Are Bees Considered Livestock for Tax Purposes (USDA & IRS)?" BootstrapBee.com, October 1, 2022, https://bootstrapbee.com/laws/are-bees-considered-livestock-tax-wise.

A NOTE FROM DR. TATIANA

Interestingly, honey bees aren't actually great pollinators–there are many types of plants they can't pollinate at all! A variety of native pollinators are far more efficient pollinators for most crops than European Honeybees, so it's better to maintain a natural habitat for native pollinators, which Angel has done at Rainmaker Farm by maintaining a native grassland area. The reason many areas depend on honeybees for pollination is that honeybees live in colonies, which means they live in large numbers in boxes handy for transportation. If your farm is in an area without a natural habitat for native pollinators, or there are pesticides that kill off insects including pollinators, you can still get your crops pollinated by hiring beekeepers to bring in loads of hives.

In Oklahoma, there are a lot of bee societies, bee people, bee clubs, and other people who are really into bees, which seemed hopeful until I actually tried to get some bees to my property. I contacted many bee people attempting to purchase bees and hire someone to help care for them. I told them I had already purchased Flow Hives. I was immediately met with resistance. Apparently in Oklahoma, the bee people are traditionalists. I was told that these newfangled Flow Hives were marketed to bee novices because they looked easy but were inferior, difficult to maintain properly, and often failed. The bee people in Oklahoma wanted nothing to do with them.

I had another problem. I couldn't get a beekeeper to come tend the bees on the farm because the farm was "too remote." Really? To me it seems like all of Oklahoma is remote, and also, isn't this what the beekeepers do, drive to places, like farms, where hives are needed and tend to the bees? I had to make dozens of calls in order to find someone willing to drive more than twenty minutes (you can't get your mail in Oklahoma without driving twenty minutes, and that's just on your own property).

The bee guy I found was recommended by a pollinator researcher at Oklahoma State University, and this guy is basically the Beethoven of Bees, except instead of composing, he knew bees. The first thing he told me was that I needed to find the perfect location for my hives, "because bees are very particular about where they live."

A NOTE FROM DR. TATIANA

It is highly unlikely that bees live in your backyard. Bees forage in your backyard and live elsewhere. Locations that are ideal for bees to seek food are not the same locations that are suitable for establishing a hive.

"No, they're not," I said. "They live in my backyard. They're not that particular. I see them all the time."

He insisted that the hives needed to be facing east, because the bees needed morning sun, and the hives needed daily shade so that the bees didn't get too hot, and the hives also needed a lot of air flow, proximity to water, and no more than a half a mile from the crops the bees were going to pollinate. These bees were prima donnas, and while I was in doubt that the bees needed any of this, I got it all done.

Then I fought with the bee guy for a while about the Flow Hives and agreed to split the difference. I got two Flow Hives and two traditional "Langstroth" hives.

THE BEE-OFF

I decided to have a bee-off and see which hive (traditional or flow) performed better. The bee guy was supposed to paint one set red and the other set blue, in honor of the Crips and Bloods, but the Beethoven of Bees painted them all pale blue (something to do with temperature control in the hives). It didn't matter. The competition was on.

I ordered the initial colonies, which the Beethoven of Bees picked up and placed in the hives so that they could build their colonies. Bees build layer by layer, and you continue adding screens to the hive, like floors in a skyscraper, to accommodate the hives' growth. The bees were thriving. Things seemed good.

And while it would seem like setting up bee real estate with all the perfect conditions would be the bee guy's biggest concern, his focus of malcontent was on the newfangled Flow Hives. Like all the bee people I met, he didn't like them.

"Are they working as well as the traditional hives?" I asked.

"Well, yes," the bee guy conceded, "but you know, they're not …" He had no real reasons, except that he had been working for years with traditional hives and had a particular way of doing things. While the hives continued to thrive, the bee guy continued to complain about the new hives.

FULL DISCLOSURE: THE FLOW HIVES

Here's the one flaw I find with the Flow Hives. I got several prominent engineers who work for my company to assemble them when they came out for the employee farm day, and they struggled. Assembling them is a challenge.

D.I.Y. Off-Grid Luxury

Long before I had to solve issues about bees, I was done waiting for the smart people and being told that new ideas were no good because they were new. Ten years ago, before I started the NPUC or dedicated my businesses to advocating for net-zero carbon dioxide emissions, I bought forty acres in Cazadero, California, from a friend who needed to sell the land. Cazadero is two hours north of San Francisco in the hills. It's a heavily forested area, sparsely populated—mainly by pot farmers living in trailers surrounded by piles of junk. It's a strange, isolated place with large lots and a general understanding that you don't go driving because you might accidentally find yourself on someone else's property and be shot when they assume you are coming to rip off their stash. It's not a great place for trick-or-treating, but it has varied topography, fantastic weather, and is generally gorgeous. I decided to take a Tier 1 action and build an off-grid home on my new property, but not any off-grid home. I wanted a luxurious hideaway. Had I bothered to ask any experts if this was possible, I likely would have been told "no" on several fronts, but I didn't bother to ask. And I didn't wait for the smart people. I am the smart people (what I don't know I am willing to learn and figure out). I got to work.

A NOTE FROM DR. TATIANA

There is a difference between "smart" and "knowledgeable." "Smart" is inherent to an individual; "knowledgeable" is about a specific topic. You can be smart and ignorant about a topic, and not smart and extremely knowledgeable about a topic. I think often when you are using smart here, you are intending "knowledgeable," "expert," or "an authority" ordained with power in a particular situation.

The land was completely undeveloped, meaning there was no infrastructure of any kind: electricity, water, roads. I had to start from scratch. If I wanted to build something, I first needed a way to get supplies onto the property, so I started trying to figure out how to build a road. I found the guy who maintained some of the dirt roads in the area. He suggested a route for a road and explained the building process, which as you may guess is more involved than it seems.

I should say that when I started this project I wasn't planning to go off-grid. I decided to go off-grid when I learned the cost of getting things on the grid. It's incredibly expensive to build utility infrastructure. In addition, in order to run utilities onto private property, you need to get a bunch of permits—California loves their permits. It would have cost me $25,000 per pole to run electricity to the property, and I would have needed four poles to reach my house. Solar power was the sustainable and cheaper option. I had learned from putting solar on my house in the Bay Area that southwest facing roofs are optimal for collecting solar power, so I picked a southwest facing spot for my new house that didn't have too much tree cover.

SAVE THE EARTH/SAVE MONEY

When I put solar on my house in the Bay Area and made other energy efficient modifications, it was not to save the earth, it was to save money. Although it saved me a little money immediately, I was not thinking about the impact it would have today or tomorrow but in a decade or more. I know I won't be able to afford the exorbitant electrical bill I foresee coming in the future. I put solar on and made adaptations now that I will have paid off by the time I retired and will have minimal bills as a retiree. It was a practical measure to preserve my way of life in the future.

I'm not a designer, nor an engineer, but that didn't stop me. I've lived in houses for a lot of my life, so I know something about them. I had also just remodeled my house in the Bay Area and had been working with a general contractor, learning about construction concerns. I used the software with which I am most familiar (PowerPoint) and got to work designing my house. I figured there would be two or three structures on the property: a main house, a guesthouse, a shed, etc. I started with the guesthouse. I designed a structure that looked somewhat like a big chicken coop with a slanted roof. I also designed a big metal shed for storage. I decided to build these two smaller structures first. As with everything that you put off, the result of that plan was that I never built a main house, and my guesthouse became the house I stay in, which works fine because I prefer not to have guests anyway.

MY MEDEVAC LANDING SITE

It doesn't make sense to build a main house now, but I did have the foundation poured in preparation. One cool thing is that the concrete pad can be used as a Medevac helicopter landing site, which—since the site is so remote it would take hours for an ambulance to arrive, if it could even find you—is good for everybody in the area.

The concrete slab also functions as an awesome dance floor.

Once I had a road in place and had designed a house that could collect solar power, I had to figure out how to get water to the property. Water is life, and besides the very tiny, only seasonal creek, there wasn't any water access on the property.

There were two options for accessing water. The first is to dig a well, which requires finding water underground (think water-witching)—which is quite a crapshoot. The other option was to catch and filter water, which seemed more possible.

MY IMPRESSION OF WATER-WITCHING

People come out with sticks and chant; nobody really knows what they're doing.

I headed back to Google and YouTube, learned all about water catchment, and designed a rain catchment system. I calculated how much water I would need annually. If I collected rainfall from the roof, I would have more water than I would need.

CALCULATE YOUR WATER USAGE

A family of four uses about one hundred gallons of water per day, or thirty-six thousand gallons per year. The roofs of my structures had the largest surface potential for catching rainfall. The guest house (turned main house) would be about 1,100 square feet. One inch of rain on a one-thousand-foot roof area is about a thousand gallons of capture. The average rainfall in Cazadero is about forty-five inches annually.

Collecting rain from the roof meant I needed to avoid using asphalt that would contaminate drinking water and opt for metal. I also learned that roofs could be designed to shed water into a gutter system that could then run to barrels. Because I like to invest now for greater benefits later, I got the biggest gutters I could find—eight inches deeper than standard gutters—with covers to keep out leaves and other debris, and five ten-thousand-gallon holding tanks to catch runoff from the house. Rain would fall on the roof and go through the gutters into the holding tank. The water would be pumped into the house from the tank nearest the house using electrical pumps.

The water that we collected would need to be safe for drinking and bathing. To prevent algae and other things from growing in the water, I made sure the tanks were UV secure so that the sun was fully blocked.

A NOTE FROM DR. TATIANA

Most algae is photosynthetic, meaning it gets its food from capturing energy from the sun, like most plants. By blocking out the sun, you prevent the growth of algae.

I also set up an automatic generator and built a little generator house behind the shed. The solar system would collect energy from the sun and store the energy in batteries. When the batteries were depleted to 20 percent, I could turn on a generator, and the generator would charge the batteries.

The generators would run on propane, which I had to get anyway because I only cook with gas. Obviously connecting a gas line to my house would have cost more than the state of California. I needed a propane tank on my property. When the propane tank company asked me how big a tank I wanted, I answered, without thinking, "Give me the biggest one you've got."

FYI: YOU CAN ALSO PUT CHLORINE IN YOUR TANKS

...to help kill anything organic (my tanks ended up being so secure that I didn't need to worry about this).

"You don't need that," the propane tank people said, which sounded to me like, "No." So my automatic response was, "You don't know what I need."

Now I have a ten-thousand-gallon propane tank parked behind my shed. The good news is that I will never, ever, ever need to refill it. The bad news is that it's absolutely ridiculous, bigger than my damn house, a clown thing that my three-bay shed, large enough to hold an RV, cannot hide. It was a bit of overkill.

BANNING GAS

Many California cities are banning gas cooking stoves from being installed in new buildings. While they are great for cooking, burning natural gas in homes and businesses contributes significantly to indoor pollution (causing asthma and related health issues) and also to greenhouse gas emissions.[58]

Once I had all the logistics figured out, I started building and moved on to more important considerations, like light fixtures and paint colors. The house has a big open feel, with no interior walls

---

58   Alex Horvath, "Federal Court Slows a California Ban on Natural Gas Appliances," Los Angeles Times, April 18, 2023, https://www.latimes.com/california/story/2023-04-17/natural-gas-debate-heats-up-as-federal-appeals-court-strikes-down-berkeley-ban.

downstairs and a wooden catwalk between the bedrooms upstairs. Because I'm a light-hog, there are huge windows and skylights everywhere. My husband-at-the-time and I had been on Safari in South Africa the previous year and had stayed in a place with a beautiful bathroom, so I created something similar complete with a soaking tub and tile shower that opens onto a deck so that I feel like I'm showering in nature. Because I love to cook, the kitchen was important. I have a Wolf stove and beautiful custom wood cabinets. There is also a metal spiral staircase in the middle (which is gorgeous but, in retrospect, a heat-suck), and an awesome fireplace (that gives off enough heat to make up for the stairs). The whole house is very energy efficient, as in it is good at retaining a comfortable temperature. Given all the wildfires, the outside of the house is concrete as a precaution; the inside is made with all the highest-grade materials, because that's how I roll. It also has a carport, extensive deck, a nice fence around seven of the acres, and I added a horse barn later. It's a fancy little two-bedroom, two-bath house.

ANGEL'S GUEST HOUSE AESTHETIC DESIGN WISH LIST:

I wanted the front door to be round—less like a portal and more like a hobbit door. I imagined a beautiful, round, stained-wood door that would sort of be the centerpiece of the house. It ends up that round doors are not very practical because, by definition, they are as tall as they are wide, which means rather than being the centerpiece, they take over the whole damn space. They're huge, super heavy, and difficult to design around. I settled instead for a big circle on the downstairs bathroom, where there is a sliding barn door.

The total cost from soup to nuts (road, structures, solar, water, propane, etc.) was less than what I would have spent to buy a house (especially with the other structures included) on the grid in this area. Making it more financially sensible is that, aside from insurance and maintenance, I have no operating costs besides maintenance.

I didn't set out to build an off-grid house. I built the house off-grid because it was pragmatic. I'm not an engineer, nor a contractor, nor a designer. I wasn't an expert on anything having to do with building a house, but I didn't wait for the smart people to solve my problems. I educated myself as necessary and unwittingly became informed about climate activity along the way. None of it was difficult. It was rudimentary; not fancy, but effective. Because I did it on my own, I mostly did it my way, with a few negotiations here and there.

No One Is Better Than You

During my youth, I met the love of my life at a ranch. I had been working on ranches since I was a child, cleaning stalls in exchange for horse riding lessons and then moving up to exercising the school horses so that they were well behaved when the paying customers came to ride. At thirteen, I went to a ranch to get a job. "I can ride anything that moves," I said to the manager. By then, that statement was true.

"Let's see what you can do," the manager said to me. He showed me three horses. "If you can break them, you can have a job."

I went into the arena, broke the three horses, and was awarded my first job. Two years later, while I was still in high school, I became foreman. It was a cattle, sheep, and dude ranch with fifty head of horse, too many cows to count, and just as many sheep—I particularly hate sheep. I was responsible for them all.

I CAN'T EMPHASIZE HOW VILE SHEEP ARE

Let me count the ways:

1. They seem to be incredibly stupid. I would routinely find them dead, having fallen into a ravine and died of drowning in rain.

2. Ranchers cut their tails off because if you don't, they just house a disgusting mess in their wool. Sheep en masse with yucky butts is a health hazard for the sheep and for anyone around them.

3. Post lamb stage, they are in no way attractive.

It was at that ranch that I learned that my greatest gift in this world is working with horses, which is unfortunate because there's no real money in it. I practiced natural horsemanship, wherein you don't use any devices like a bridal, halter, or saddle. What you have instead is communication with the horse. The horse learns to feel what you're thinking by the way your weight shifts: When you want to turn, you unconsciously turn your head; you think, "I want to go over there, your eyes shift your head slightly, and the horse feels the shift and turns in the direction you are looking."

One of those three horses that I'd had to break to get my first job on that ranch was a pony named Sandy. I have often referred to her as my soulmate in fur. She was an interesting horse. Previously I had dreamed of owning a beautiful, black war horse that I would head off with into the sunset. He was huge and masculine. But we don't choose who we fall in love with.

Sandy and I were together for the next twenty-two years. The way that I took her from the ranch when I left the job was akin to stealing but absolutely necessary. In the next decade, I did not really have the means nor the lifestyle to have a horse, but I always figured it out.

We had a lot of adventures together—once run over by a helicopter, another time plunging off a cliff into a lake.

At one point I was living the life of a surfer and sleeping in a box car with Sandy tied out back. I got into an argument with the guy who owned the property and had to leave in the middle of the night. I packed everything I owned into my $250 car with two gears that didn't work. I had to take Sandy with me, but of course, I didn't have a horse trailer. There weren't many options, and I needed to make it happen. I tied a lead from Sandy's harness to the bumper of my car and drove fifteen miles down into the foothills of Sacramento on the highway with Sandy trotting along behind me. It was an unconventional solution, but it worked.

HOW I MET DR. TATIANA

I met Tatiana because she had a horse that she boarded at the same place where I boarded Sandy. [Tatiana added text: It was a place on county land, where you entered a lottery to get in and cared for the horses as part of a collective to keep costs down.] Tatiana and I both come from very low-income upbringings, and in our twenties, we had both ended up with horses we had had for a decade and were scraping around trying to figure out how to pay for their many expenses. It's a particularly strange and unique endeavor, and Tatiana and I met while taking on that challenge.

Take Action: Be the Smart People

Consider this to be your pep talk: You are the solution. Stop waiting for someone else to arrive with answers. You are the person who can identify the problem; you are the person who can find a resolution; you are the person who can take action, you are the person who can be open to change, you are the smart people; you are the authority; you can become the expert. You are the person who can recognize what needs to be fixed and fix it.

I am not a scientist, nor an architect, nor a farmer, and you also do not need to be. You do not need a PhD, or to be a CEO, or to have money. If I leave the human race with one kernel of knowledge, it's simply that no one is better than you. You are as good as you need to be to do the things that need to be done. What you need is awareness, education, a can-do attitude, and the initiative to get started. Here are some things you can do now.

GET EDUCATED

Education is everywhere and often free. Look for:

- Free classes and seminars online
- Courses or lectures at universities or other educational institutions
- Google
- YouTube
- Podcasts
- Talking to people with experience (from all different perspectives) to gain knowledge about a variety of topics
- Trial and error

Tier 1: The Savvy At-Home Composter

1. Look up that environmentally friendly household project that you've been thinking about but haven't figured out yet. Figure it out and get started.
2. Take action to align your lifestyle with environmentally conscious concepts and strategies where you can.

3. Talk about these concepts at parties, backyard BBQs, school events with your friends and fellow parents. Teach them about what you are doing. Learn from them about what they are doing.

Tier 2: The CEO Environmental Powerhouse

1. Time to do what you do best: Inspire your leadership teams and subsequent teams to develop or enhance your ESG market strategy and then EXECUTE. This is not a death by meeting situation, this is pure action. You will make mistakes, and they may cost money, consider it an investment in positioning for what lies ahead.
2. Do all the stuff the Savvy At-Home Composter is doing.

Tier 3: The Big Cheese World Changer

1. If you have made it this far in the book, you know exactly what you are going to do. Now clear your schedule where needed, connect with the real doers on your teams, and begin.
2. Do all the stuff the CEO Environmental Powerhouse is doing.
3. Do all the stuff the Savvy At-Home Composter is doing.

CHAPTER 8

Broad Reach

Snacks and Other Essentials

Before I started Rainmaker Farm, or built an off-grid getaway, I was just a Tier 1: Savvy At-Home Composter chick trying to be less destructive to the environment. I was gardening my brains out, composting, recycling, and doing every other hippie thing that I could think of, but I wanted to make more of an impact.

I had a wider reach than my home—I own companies that employ around a hundred people. I could change things at work. My companies had a calculable carbon footprint in the same way I had my own. I could reduce or eliminate the ways that my businesses directly and indirectly emitted greenhouse gases. I needed to move up to Tier 2: CEO Environmental Powerhouse.

Something I've learned about running a company is that snacks are extremely important. In addition to keeping employees from getting hangry, snacks make employees feel valued (it's amazing how a complimentary bag of Cheetos can improve the relationship between an employee and her company). A company can increase an employee's workload, introduce stupid dress codes, accelerate deadlines, and all of these things may cause employees to grumble, but if you stop providing snacks, they will revolt. In all of my

A NOTE FROM DR. TATIANA

Leaders of organizations have known for centuries that providing food and food security is a powerful way to keep groups of people united.

offices, we provide nice snacks. We have sparkling and still water, soda, wine, beer (as you would guess, all of my offices have full bars), chips, cookies, nut mixes, etc. Before I decided to make my offices green, we were serving snacks and beverages in single-use plastics. No more. I decided that the office would only provide reusable or recyclable containers. We found beverages

> "An army, like a serpent, goes upon its belly,"
>
> – **Frederic of Prussia**[59]

in glass bottles and aluminum cans and bought chips (everyone loves chips) in large quantities and filled reusable lidded containers with fancy metal scoops. All of this dramatically cut down on the amount of waste produced in the office.

WAYS THAT RUNNING A BUSINESS IS LIKE RUNNING A DAYCARE

- Snack time (obviously) and other comforts that have nothing to do with the purpose of your endeavors but are about cajoling human beings enough to get some base level of activity out of them.
- Managing small, personal conflicts that essentially amount to both sides saying, "Mine" or "She did it first."
- Naps (people taking them or obviously needing them)
- Telling people several times to "clean up" their mess ...
- Routinely fielding requests that begin with, "Can I have ..."
- Drop-off and pick-up time coordination
- Finding dirty dishes/wrappers everywhere

Next, I found a composting program where we could collect most of the remaining waste—all the snacks employees didn't finish. This may sound complicated, but it was relatively simple. We already had recycling bins beside the bins marked "landfill." We now added "composting" bins.

---

59   Jakob Walter and Marc Raeff, The Diary of a Napoleonic Foot Soldier, (Windrush, 1999).

ZERO WASTE AT SFO

In San Francisco, many highly commercial establishments (including the airport) now have this three-separation model for dealing with waste.[60]

Then, because we were creating compost, I decided to start a garden at work, which meant that months later my employees were taking home fresh tomatoes and basil—a perk akin to great snacks and an open bar. My offices were looking very green, and while I couldn't go into all of my employees' houses and make sure they were recycling at home (because that would be creepy and possibly illegal), I had discovered a direct path to influence how my employees interacted with the world while they were at work.

GREEN TEMPORARY OFFICES

...are fully equipped and furnished office spaces that are designed in an environmentally conscious way that you can lease for a week or a year. They have recycling and composting programs, and they are energy efficient. They also allow you to get space when you need it rather than building or buying a space that you will only use sporadically. These have worked great for Motive Power teams that sometimes need to locate to another part of the country or world for a few months while working on a project.

60   Zero Waste Case Study: San Francisco International Airport (SFO)."
      EPA, May 11, 2023. https://www.epa.gov/transforming-waste-tool/
      zero-waste-case-study-san-francisco-international-airport-sfo.

In order to help my employees reduce their carbon footprints outside of the office, I created incentives that supported environmentally conscious decisions: I subsidized mass transit and offered to contribute $2,500 toward a down payment on any electric car. I also began a kind of a grassroots educational force, which is to say I started talking about being environmentally conscious at work and explaining why the office was no longer using single-use products and instead composting banana peels and growing tomatoes. Those conversations spiraled outward until they were a part of every conversation we had at work in some way. An environmentally conscious viewpoint became part of company culture, changed the work dynamic, and ultimately brought people back to a natural equation where they were aware of and in line with nature. It felt prosperous, connected people, and dedicated employees in a new way to my company.

I started a formal green group in the company for employees who wanted to meet together to shoot ideas around about other environmentally conscious actions that we could take (and have a few drinks). I learned about cloth napkins, dryer balls, refillable soap, and sheet laundry detergent—all ideas that I took home.

MY REVIEW OF ENVIRONMENTALLY CONSCIOUS PRODUCTS

Cloth Napkins ★ ★ ★ ★

These are so multi-useful! In your mind think of someone giving you ten cents for every paper towel you don't use. It is a game changer OVERNIGHT.

Reusable Grocery Bags ★ ★ ★ ★ ★

I have about forty-five of these, and I use them for absolutely everything—laundry, grocery, sports equipment, wine, and everything else.

Refillable Soaps ★ ★ ★ ★ ★

Method is my brand of choice. It is so satisfying to know that you are reducing plastic so dramatically while simultaneously making multicolor swirls in your dish soap. They have liquids of all types and live by the creed: People against Dirty.

Countertop Compost Bins ★ ★ ★ ★ ★

This little device is in CONSTANT use in my house. No smell and easy to clean.

Water Efficient Toilets ★

These are crappy, as in when you press the button, the mess doesn't go away, so you press the button again and again until eventually you've used more water than you would have used flushing a regular toilet once.

And of course ...

All-Electric Vehicles ★ ★ ★ ★ ★

Who doesn't like driving spaceships??? My computer on wheels knows more about where I am going than I do.

Bringing the green movement to work had significantly lowered the carbon footprint of my offices, increased communication, and united employees in a mission with the company. Engaging my employees in ESG actions gave them practical, intentional experience in something that is often the focus of our consulting work, thereby making them better able to communicate with clients. Another triple (or quadruple) win. I was on a roll, and I knew that my influence could extend beyond my office.

A Brief Lesson on the GHG Protocol Decarbonization Scopes

The Greenhouse Gas (GHG) Protocol was established by the World Resources Institute (WRI) and the World Business Council for Sustainable Development (WBCSD) along with advisors from governments, businesses, organizations, and industry leaders. The purpose of the protocol is to create internationally standardized and recognized frameworks for measuring and managing greenhouse gas emissions.[61] The GHG Protocol now offers the most internationally recognized and used greenhouse gas calculating tools and accounting standards.[62]

The GHG protocol defines three scopes that classify greenhouse gas emissions types, making it easier for companies and individuals to understand how their actions contribute to greenhouse gas emissions. The scopes are sort of like ripples created when a pebble is dropped into a puddle, the effects radiating out from you or your businesses starting with those greenhouse gases that you are directly responsible for (Scope 1) due to the fossil fuels you burn to run an office or make a product and ranging to those that you are indirectly responsible for (Scopes 2 and 3) because you purchased goods and services that emitted greenhouse gases in their creation or because the products or services that you offer create greenhouse gas emissions when used by consumers. If the scopes were applied to theft, Scope 1 would be like committing robbery, Scope 2 would be like hiring someone to commit robbery, and Scope 3 would be like knowingly buying the goods obtained in a robbery on the cheap. (In this example, theft is bad, just to be clear.)

---

61   "About Us," About Us | Greenhouse Gas Protocol, accessed September 12, 2022, https://ghgprotocol.org/about-us.

62   "Standards," Standards | Greenhouse Gas Protocol, accessed September 12, 2022, https://ghgprotocol.org/standards.

To be more specific:

Scope 1 Direct Emissions: These are often the obvious things that we think of, things that you or your company do that directly cause greenhouse gas emissions like the burning of fossil fuels or the release of greenhouse gases on site.[63] For example:

Use of natural gas to heat the office.

The operation of business-owned trucks or vehicles.

Coolant leakage from refrigerators (that cause the release of greenhouse gases).

Production that results in the release of greenhouse gases.

Scope 2: Indirect Emissions: These are the emissions that you or your company are complicit in causing by purchasing energy created off site.[64] For example:

Greenhouse gas emissions from the utility company from whom you purchase electricity.

Scope 3: Indirect Emissions (created upstream or downstream of a company's production) not included in Scope 2: This includes the emissions of all the parties associated with helping a business to run. Scope three is the most difficult to measure and also represents the lion's share of greenhouse gas emissions for most businesses.[65] For example:

Emissions from producing and shipping products used to create products.

Emissions from disposing of packaging from products by the consumer.

Emissions created by employees commuting to and from work.

63 Tara Bernoville, "What Are Scopes 1, 2, and 3 of Carbon Emissions?" Plan A Academy, June 12, 2022. Retrieved November 1, 2022, from https://plana.earth/academy/what-are-scope-1-2-3-emissions.

64 Ibid.

65 Ibid.

The Hyphenated Role of the CEO

Corporations have to save the world (I'm especially talking to you Tier 2: CEO Environmental Powerhouses). It won't be the government alone. The government does not act quickly; corporations act quickly. CEOs are problem solvers adept at adapting to short- and long-term changes in their industries. Where other people see crisis, entrepreneurs and CEOs see opportunity.

Also, most CEOs (and especially entrepreneurs) are versatile. We are not afraid to wear multiple hats . Have you seen some of the creative uses of the hyphen on LinkedIn profiles? Owner-founder-CEO-Head of Scheduling-Financial Administrator-Catering Advisor-Internal Gallery Curator … We are the one-man/woman bands of the business world. I can hyphenate with the best of them, so I decided to branch out in order to make Motive Power's environmentally consciousness values available to other businesses, starting with the ones we work with, and we work with many.

I did this because I was on a mission but also because it was good for my business. Motive Power and 10/6 Professional Services work with large organizations on organizational development, change adoption, and data innovation. We drive systems implementations of various kinds, which means that we really drive the companies for whom we work. I decided that Motive Power and 10/6 Professional Services were going to move to the

Angel wearing multiple hats

Tier 3: Big Cheese World Changer level and be on the forefront of private industry in the environmentally conscious movement, earning a reputation for helping clients become ESG compliant and showing them how to market those good choices to their benefit.

My logic for deciding to be a leader for private industry in the environmentally conscious movement was simple: as the ESG climate heats up—all puns intended—companies need help adapting to environmental and social changes, and adopting ESG standards is the natural path to stay current, profitable, and in compliance. When change adaptations are ESG focused, they can be holistically transformative, socially impactful, and measurably influential, all while reinforcing quality on multiple levels. Who doesn't want to get on board with that? Companies are looking for ways to associate themselves with good actions and establish positive reputations. They recognize their deficiencies in understanding and addressing ESG issues. They are looking for the smart people who can help them get on track and catch the wave; that's where my consultants could come in. We would become the smart people.

I began an informal and formal education campaign. I started at Tier 2. Informally I talked to my employees (and anyone willing to listen) about our new policies and aggressively offered people fresh veggies from the company garden. Formally I designed and created an entire series of ESG-related courses that were both mandatory and free for my employees so that they had a clear understanding of ESG issues and the function of ESG compliance in business. I taught my employees to approach every project with an ESG focus and prepared them to communicate effectively with clients about ESG issues and solutions.

THE ACCIDENTAL FORTUNE

I once mentioned the video courses to someone in banking.

"That's what we need," she said. "Are they available for purchase?"

They are not, but they could be. Or someone in the banking industry who was trained and knowledgeable in ESG could produce a series of ESG courses for that industry. Anyone in any industry could do this, market the courses, and make a ton of money.

Now all of my employees were educated about science and policy issues around climate change issues (making them the smart people), behaving in green ways at work (giving them practical experience), encouraged to make Tier 1 environmentally conscious decisions at home (a nudge to genuinely embrace an environmental mindset), and structuring their relationships with clients around ESG compliance (most were also excited about the direction and proselytizing to friends, family, neighbors, and strangers at the grocery store).

ANOTHER TRIPLE WIN

This is much more than a triple win for Motive Power. The green movement at work helps to

1. Build and solidify company culture by helping employees feel like they are a part of something unified and larger than themselves, all of which helps with employee retention;

2. I can advertise our green movement with pictures of our vegetable garden, which is great for PR and bringing in clients; and

3. The movement has created products, like the ESG courses for employees, that are marketable.

I was ready to export my environmental sensibility to my clients. I couldn't go into my clients' offices and replace all their single-use plastics with reusable containers, but I could invite them to my office, talk about what I was doing, and make them aware of what was possible on a structural level—an action more widely impactful than swapping out their single-use plastics. I could also prepare my employees to represent (and hopefully internalize) the same sensibility.

I could also set environmentally conscious standards for Motive Power's interactions with clients. As consultants, one of our biggest contributions to greenhouse gas is travel. We fly all over the place to meet with clients and to work on projects. I decided that, whenever possible, my employees would only take direct flights. As I mentioned earlier, most fuel is used during takeoff, so direct flights emit less greenhouse gas. Our clients foot the bill for these flights, and direct flights are often more expensive, so this could potentially piss people off, but I had an angle—that is to say, I had an honest way to present the situation as a triple win for clients. Armed with charts, projects, fresh tomatoes, and later pictures of Rainmaker Farm, I started talking to our clients about their new triple win. Rather than saving a buck by having our consultants change planes three times to get across the country, they should invest money in direct flights and participate in an environmentally conscious choice. They would be 1) contributing less to greenhouse gas emissions (which I could show with my carbon footprint calculations); 2) benefit from marketing their environmental choice; and 3) get more bang for their buck from my consultants who could work more consistently on long flights than they would wandering through airports.

Whatever your business, it is easy to see how adopting an ESG focus can be beneficial, and equally easy to make arguments to your clients for adopting ESG-focused decisions. Ultimately these decisions have to do with resistance mitigation and preparing for long-term change in ways that are sustainable rather than superficial. In other words, it is a good investment. Motive Power and 10/6 Professional Services found a way to meet a need and provide strategies to prepare companies for environmental and social changes and to capitalize on those changes.

But outreach to clients and shifting their focus to an ESG lens has a bigger payback. Most people embrace this change—people in every walk of life have an innate desire to return to something that is in balance. It feels prosperous. When we make companies feel good about the work that they're doing, they also feel good about the work we are doing for them. It's reciprocal. In several instances, I have targeted businesses with efforts to initiate environmentally conscious practices, and these efforts have resulted in a change in mindset. They are inspired by doing good. Inspired clients are loyal clients and are often motivated to spread that new environmentally conscious mindset across social paradigms and within multiple industries.

Walking Our Talk

But I had a farther reach even than my employees or our existing clients. I could use my mission to connect other people and organizations to one another in ways that would benefit me and my goals. One of the most successful ways that I did this was by moving up to Tier 3 and becoming a Big Cheese World Changer through the creation of the NPUC. I created a networking path between utilities because I work with utilities, but anyone could do this for any industry.

BECOME AN INDUSTRY THOUGHT LEADER

When you make the effort to create a network like the NPUC, you and your companies reap the benefits of being at the center of that network, responsible for facilitating communications that (here's the triple win):

1. Contribute to a greater good, which in turn

2. gleans you the reputation of being a thought leader in the space, which in turn

3. equates to more and better business opportunities for your companies.

Forming the NPUC was a way of walking my talk. Motive Power's most successful networking comes out of action: walking our talk. We are engaged in all the practices that we promote. We are leading by example. People notice what we do and want to be involved. One of the most visible ways that Motive Power walks our talk is Rainmaker Farm. By actually transforming the farm from traditional to regenerative farming, rather than philosophizing about what types of farms are best, we are walking our talk. This has helped us connect to people and build networks. It gives us hands-on knowledge of the industry and the challenge practitioners face and proves that our beliefs are genuine. And it gets people's attention—everyone loves to hear about the adventures of a San Francisco Bay Area CEO in rural Oklahoma, and regenerative farming is generally inspirational. Rainmaker Farm not only produces crops, but it also creates experiences that in turn birth stories that spread informally during happy hour and formally through short films and reports. Farmers from the Heartland and businesspeople from the West Coast can connect over the tangible, practical elements of farming, the physical labor of planting, and the beauty of being immersed in the natural world. It bridges political, social, and economic divides and acts as a hopeful neutralizer that shifts the conversation from debate to collaboration.

Actions like these help spread our environmental message by word of mouth. I often say that I hire people for their big brains and their big mouths. I need them to be smart; I need them to speak up; I need them to set an example. My employees are my largest networking asset. They talk to their families, their friends, and complete strangers about the environmental mission of my companies and the related actions they are taking. And they talk to our current and potential clients. I invest a great deal of time and funding into informing, educating, and exciting my employees about the mission of our company because these issues matter to me, and I know that my efforts will have a domino effect for my company and beyond.

HERE'S ANOTHER ANGEL SAYING

We have a saying at Motive Power: "Good work gets good work." It has proven true. I met a woman the other day who had heard about Rainmaker Farm and the Gulch Environmental Foundation.

"I want come and volunteer my time," she said. "When can I come? Where do I sign up?"

People want to be a part of the conversation and the movement—they see good work and want to help. Other CEOs, industry leaders, and potential clients see the power of that enthusiasm—they see good work and want to employ our services and give us more good work. By acting in environmentally conscious and ESG-compliant ways, we attract clients and naturally build networks.

All Our Patent Are Belong to You

In 2014, Elon Musk released its electric motor schematics to the world to be duplicated. In a blog post on Tesla's website titled "All Our Patent Are Belong to You," Musk wrote, "Yesterday, there was a wall of Tesla patents in the lobby of our Palo Alto headquarters. That is no longer the case. They have been removed, in the spirit of the open source movement, for the advancement of electric vehicle technology."[66] He did this in part because he believed that "the world would all benefit from a common, rapidly-evolving technology platform."[67] He had an idea, put that idea to work—setting an example, then released information so that others could follow.

I had promoted indirect outreach to communities beyond my employees, clients, and the utility industry through word of mouth and the demonstration of Motive Power's actions, but like Elon Musk, I could also perform more direct outreach to a broader public. I did this with the NPUC by publishing the Decarbonization Report. The Decarbonization Report not only offers data that you cannot find collected and consolidated elsewhere, but the report also presents the data in a highly digestible way with cool infographics and bite-size soundbite information that move research about the utility industry into the marketing realm. The Decarbonization Report is compelling not only to utilities but also to stakeholders; stakeholders in the utility community are everyone. The rate payers are also regulators, educators, the government, and investors—even Bill Gates pays an electric bill. Motive Power made the Decarbonization Report free and available. Because the report can be widely distributed (as a downloadable PDF) and used for various purposes by different audiences, it is

---

66   Elon Musk, "All Our Patent Are Belong to You," Tesla, accessed November 17, 2022, https://www.tesla.com/blog/all-our-patent-are-belong-you.

67   Ibid.

and will continue to be referenced by organizations and leaders from different industries.

The Gulch Environmental Foundation also intends to release a publication for a large audience. This will be similar to Musk's release of the Tesla patents in that it will be a playbook of how exactly Rainmaker Farm transitioned a conventional farm to a regenerative farm including the associated costs, successes and failures, and alternative options that prospective farmers might want to consider. With the release of the playbook, other organizations, companies, individual people, and you will not only be able to see what we're doing. This means you will have step-by-step instructions about how you can do it too.

Robots at Rainmaker

As I was writing this book, my daughter, who is in eighth grade, came to me and said, "It would be so cool if I could bring my robotics class out to the farm."

I had gone to her robotics conference in a sweatshirt with a Gulch Environmental Foundation logo. Later the kids looked up the logo, learned about the farm, got inspired by the project, and talked to my daughter.

Farms and robotics may seem like disparate subjects, but farms can be very roboticized—like Roomba level, set it and go. Actually the agricultural industry (like other industries) is turning into a robotics industry. My farm is only a little roboticized. I have a super drone, that I was happy to let my daughter's class drive around, especially if they could get it running correctly. Drones have become very useful on farms in many ways. I hoped to use my drone to survey my land. A parcel can be divided into a grid pattern allowing a drone to collect specific information about soil content and growth patterns. It's incredibly useful for understanding what is working and what is needed in different areas over different seasons. I was thrilled that my daughter's robotics class might come and take a look at my drone.

ROBOTS ON FARMS CAN

- Milk cows *(https://farm.kbs.msu.edu/pdc/robotic-milking/)*
- Select and harvest ripe fruit *(https://www.tortugaagtech.com)*
- Space container crops *(https://www.public.harvestai.com)*
- Identify and remove weeds via AI and laser *(https://carbonrobotics.com)*
- Mow *(https://www.scytherobotics.com)*
- Use AI to monitor an individual plant's moisture level and deliver water and nutrients to meet specific needs (https://ironox.com/technology/)

"Let's get them to the farm," I said.

My daughter is a lot like me, kind of hardcore and go-getter-y, but she looked at me with wide-eyed mysticism and said, "Do you think we could really do that?"

I said, "Who are you talking to? I can do anything."

She said, "Yeah, you can do anything."

In September 2022 my daughter's class flew out to Oklahoma, had a day at the farm, and conducted a class in robotics for any interested kid in the vicinity. Not only was my daughter's class excited but all my neighbors in Oklahoma were also raring to go. Many of the local farmers agreed to reach out to local teachers. (Since every farmer is either married to a schoolteacher or has a daughter who grew up to be a schoolteacher, they didn't need to make many phone calls.) Matt, the local farmer who works with Rainmaker Farm, agreed to discuss soil samples with the class, my other neighbor prepared a presentation on cattle, and Dr. Tatiana came to talk to the class about the science-y side of energy. I knew the farmers were excited about the kids coming to the farm because the week before the kids came, they started texting me pictures of cows. The morning the class showed up, they lectured me, via text, when I mistakenly texted back, "happy cows," when the pictured individuals were, in fact, calves.

I planned a whole day on the farm for my daughter's class. I worked the kids in the morning: planting trees, picking up garbage, spreading hay as mulch. Then fed them lunch and let them play a little cornhole before the presentations began. We met some cows, drove by the bees, and talked about soil. Then we had local kids who belonged to a robotics club at their high school join us for an interactive robotics demonstration on the farm. It was a great day. The local farmers were excited, the kids were happy, and my daughter was a rock-star host. We got a lot done, initiated some great conversations, and showed people how to be more environmentally conscious. At the end of the day, the two robotics teams exchanged information and vowed to keep in touch.

After my daughter's class left the farm, Dr. Tatiana and I stayed, along with some of the farmers and community members who were still excited about the field trip. The next day was Sunday, and one of my neighbors invited Dr. Tatiana and me to church. We went for two reasons. The main reason was that the person who invited us was the ninety-five-year-old grandmother of the neighbors with whom we had been working most closely, and she drove her truck all the way to the farm to invite us, with a bad hip. I'm traditional in this respect; if an elderly woman asks me to do something (even without the drive and bad hip), I happily do it. The other reason we went is that in small towns, like the one where Rainmaker Farm is situated in Oklahoma, much of community life revolves around the church. We wanted to show our respect for and connect to the community by participating in what matters to our neighbors there. I recognize that I do things a little differently than they do things and that they've been open, patient, and welcoming. I wanted the community to know that I appreciate them, respect them, and that I want to be a part of what's going on there.

THIS HAPPENED

She was not even the oldest person I met that day. After church, a man introduced himself to me.

"Hi, welcome to town. I'm a neighbor, there's anything you ever need, I'm right around the corner," he said, getting up to come and shake my hand.

He looked eighty, but he had just turned one hundred. He told me the town had thrown a parade for him on his birthday. "I didn't really see the reason for it all," he told me. "I didn't do anything. I just got old."

He asked me to put my information in his iPhone so that we could keep in touch. He was interested in Rainmaker Farm's transition to a regenerative farm and also interested in the way I was educating kids and other people about farming. We talked for a long time. He told me he was a World War II vet, shot down twice, prisoner of war. Really an incredible person. He definitely deserved the parade.

To be clear, I'm a flaming atheist. Dr. Tatiana is Jewish by heritage, but not all that into it from the religious aspect. We showed up with bells on to the small, well-kept church. It was 1960s aesthetic with wood-paneled walls and a welcoming feel. There was a pulpit in the front, a piano to the side, rows of wooden pews, and fold-out tables in the back. Dr. Tatiana and I took our places in the back pew. There was singing, standing up and sitting down, kids fidgeting in the row in front of us, and reading from the Bible. The ninety-five-year-old neighbor who invited us was the pianist, and she knew what she was doing. In the middle of the service, she stopped the sermon to introduce us to the congregation. We stood again. After the service, many attendees came up to introduce themselves and welcome us to the community. The whole thing was kind of wonderful.

The sermon started with a talk about sin, which I happen to know something about. Then the preacher told stories from the Bible that had to do with David. David was the son of a farmer and shepherd who proved himself by slaying Goliath and later became a king. His great achievement was uniting all the tribes of Israel. It seemed an apropos finale to our farm day.

Back at home in California, my daughter's school was already calling to plan their next farm day. They wanted to expand the program. The trip had been great but too short. They wanted to stay for longer, bring more classes, and ultimately have more exposure.

"Can we do that?" they asked.

"We can do anything," I said.

Take Action: Make an Impact

The environment is changing, and as a business owner or employee, you can also find ways to capitalize on being on the forefront of the environmentally conscious movement within your industry. I chose to form the NPUC and work with utilities because energy generation is one of the biggest sources of greenhouse gas emissions, and many of the ways to decarbonize other sectors of the economy depend on the decarbonization of the energy utilities. I chose to work with utilities because I knew that I could make a big impact with my efforts.

Whether you have influence over a small community, a single office, multiple corporations, or entire industries, you can similarly use your time and efforts wisely to make an impact and get the biggest bang for your buck. Assess the problems in your domain, find a solution, and implement the solution that will give you a triple win.

Tier 1: The Savvy At-Home Composter

Recognize that your voice is most trusted in groups you are already part of, so be sure to reach out about environmental issues and actions in which you are interested. Use your word of mouth, and little by little you can influence positive change.

Envision yourself retired, or if you are retired play along: What can you do to minimize waste and thus minimize cost? Get rid of waste: clothes waste, food waste, energy waste, water waste, etc. ("waste not, want not").

THE LEFTOVERS

Learn to enjoy and remake leftovers, reducing food waste is huge. There is even a reality show about it on Netflix called Best Leftovers Ever! that inspires new dishes from yesterday's meals.

Tier 2: The CEO Environmental Powerhouse

1. Participate in ESG reporting for your companies and be aware of up-and-coming federal, state, and local regulations that will likely affect your industries. Soon ESG reporting and compliance will likely be as mandatory as paying your taxes.
2. Consider moving to a different corporate designation (like B corp), which allows for new market positioning. It also feels good to be alongside the notable firms like Patagonia, Method, and other B corps.

3. Institute formal and informal education in the workplace that help employees recognize the benefits of ESG compliance and environmentally conscious actions.

4. Institute environmentally conscious programs (composting, recycling, regulations about single-use containers in the office) at your workplace, as well as those that incentivize your employees to take environmentally conscious action outside of the office (by using mass transit, direct flights, or making electric car purchases). Find actions that are sustainable as well as those that suit your culture (for Motive Power this was things like the UN Sustainability Program, but there are MANY others).

5. Recruit talent for mission-driven capability. Ensure that those you hire align with your mindset and approaches on climate impact.

6. Recognize whom you have the power to influence by marketing your ESG compliant choices (this may be clients, business partners, or other businesses with whom you work).

7. Do all the stuff the Savvy At-Home Composter is doing.

Tier 3: The Big Cheese World Changer

1. Take and invest in environmentally conscious actions and make these actions visible to a wide public including a detailed account of what you are doing, how you are doing it, and the impact it has on the environment.

2. Review Environmental, Social, and Governance (ESG) Greenhouse Gases (GHG) Scopes 1–3 and ensure that all of your companies, and those that you invest in, are managing their direct emissions, indirect emissions, and their supply chain carbon footprint accordingly.

3. Ensure your organizations have a prospective on Scopes 1–3 and create or update associated reporting.
4. Don't just network, be the Network Creator.
5. Do all the stuff the CEO Environmental Powerhouse is doing.
6. Do all the stuff the Savvy At-Home Composter is doing.

CHAPTER 9

Connection

The Clown and the Queen

William Shakespeare almost always included a character in his plays who acted as the fool. These fools were usually court jesters, or otherwise overlooked figures, who were in proximity to people of great power. Because it was the job of the jester to poke fun at royalty and entertain, the jester was uniquely positioned to be at the center of everyone's attention with a license to say whatever the hell he wanted—because he is the clown, he can get away with insulting the queen. While the people of the court were outwardly laughing and making light of the insults the jester espoused, they were also internalizing the truths that he revealed. By the end of the play, it was obvious to the audience (and often the other characters) that the fool was not a fool at all. He had used his playful position to ease tension with the other characters so that he could speak to them honestly and help to advance the plot.

Not only did these fools get away with a whole ton of shit, but they also wove into their jokes political sentiment that appealed to a wide audience. Jesters interacted with people of all walks of life: They often performed at ceremonies that were open to the entire kingdom from scrub maid to the king himself. The good ones could make jokes that hit home, in different ways, to everyone present. The fools were masters of connecting with all sorts of people. And the fool connected people to one another. The fool made a joke or played a prank, and everyone laughed together—often at the fool's expense. The fool didn't mind everyone laughing at him so long as he had succeeded in his goal of starting a conversation about something significant.

MY FAVORITE SHAKESPEAREAN FOOLS

Touchstone from As You Like It
Amid a bunch of family in-fighting over power, Touchstone makes astute and sometimes brutal commentary about the other characters and allies himself with the protagonists, whom he helps win the day.

The Fool from King Lear
Poised in the position of trusted advocate to the king, the Fool is also able to tell hard truths (including pointing out the king's faults) softened by humor and sarcasm.

Feste from Twelfth Night
Hired by the countess, Olivia, for entertainment, Feste is allowed to say anything (things no one else can say) in the name of a good joke.

Puck from A Midsummer Night's Dream
Employed as the jester to the king, Puck is no fool and moves to the foreground of the story to, in my opinion, steal the show.

I'm happy to be the fool, to be the joke at the business meeting in the fancy restaurant who pulls out a hippie bag of tricks, or the CEO from California who shows up on the farm thinking she can move a two-ton tire. I'm happy to be the butt of the joke. Everyone can come together to laugh at how ridiculous I am, and while I have their attention, I'll do and say things that might disrupt their thinking. I embrace the ridicule that starts the conversation.

Learning to connect to people and connect people to one another is the battle when it comes to making change. This has always been the case in all things: war, running a company, helping a community thrive—for absolutely anything. Connection is what moves the world.

If we want change, we must first learn to connect to people. For me, the best way to connect is to realize that I am people too—to be vulnerable and fallible. I want to be accessible to both peasants and royalty. Or more than accessible, like the jester, I want everyone to feel that the message of my joke was made especially for him or her.

What Drives You

In 2022, Ford announced the 2023 release of F-150 Lightning, an all-electric, full-size truck. It was not marketed like a Prius that boasts energy efficiency for socially conscious liberal consumers who want to use their purchasing power to make environmental impacts; nor was it marketed like a Tesla that represents itself as a high-performance luxury sportscar connected to a fleet of energy efficient products for the wealthy and elite. Rather, Ford F-150 Lightning is marketed to typical Ford truck owners: a practical, Middle-America, working-class population who have livelihoods to protect, just need to get the job done, and don't have time to consider either the aerodynamics or environmental implications of some fancy electric thing. It is a brilliant campaign.

Big Impact

The F-150 (the nonelectric version) has been the best-selling vehicle in the US for four decades. Choosing this model as the one to make all-electric has the potential to make a big impact on the automobile industry and the environment.[68]

F-150 Lightning's introductory advertisement starts with close-ups of the truck's sleek exterior and then moves to a desert

---

68 Sean Tucker, "Ford F-150 Was Not America's Best-selling Vehicle in Second Quarter ..." Kelly Blue Book: The Trusted Resource, July 12, 2021, accessed December 30, 2022, https://www.kbb.com/car-news/ford-f-150-was-not-americas-best-selling-vehicle-in-second-quarter/.

landscape in the evening. Lightning (the kind that happens when negative charges clouds are attracted to positive charges in the ground) flashes on a lone road. Two bright headlights navigate the curves.

LIGHTNING IS A BRILLIANT TITLE

- Lightning as in natural power, a spark of electricity between two elements in the atmosphere, or the atmosphere and the ground.
- Lightning as in discovery via Ben Franklin and a kite.
- Lighting as an adjective meaning extremely fast.

The monologue begins, "Can a truck change everything?"[69] But now, rather than droning on about climate change, fossil fuel addiction, and getting to net-zero carbon dioxide emissions over shots of waterfalls and deer leaping in forests, the ad moves into a Ford factory where workers in hardhats guide parts together. The monologue continues talking about change from an entirely utilitarian perspective: what technology can do for you, what truck drivers will need in the future, and transforming manufacturing. The announcer answers his own question, starting not with how electric cars will change our environmental impact, but how they will change the Ford company.

"It can change the way we build forever, creating state-of-the-art, zero waste-to-landfill facilities that change communities and regions along the way. It can change how Americans, how the world, feels about electric cars. It can change who we think drives a truck, who drives an EV."[70]

69 Ford, Ford Motor Company, "Can a Truck Change Everything? | F-150 Lightning | Ford," YouTube, April 26, 2022, https://www.youtube.com/watch?v=KDptc0ycLhc.

70 Ibid.

A montage of shots shows the F-150 Lightning whipping around in the mud, splashing through a river, bouncing across rocks, the bed being filled with lumber (all the standard tough-guy moves Ford uses to show that its trucks are powerful and can take anything), and a final shot of a peaceful country road where the truck effortlessly pulls an oversized trailer. It is a machine. A tool. Tough. Rugged. Utilitarian.

The word "electric" is barely mentioned ("EV" is substituted most times), and while natural landscapes sometimes fill the background, these are present to show F-150 Lightning's command of an untamed world, not to suggest that it is preserving the land over which it travels. In the PR campaign for F-150 Lightning, Ford ditches the green narrative around which most of our discussions of electric cars are based and replaces it with a consumer-focused argument: This truck is better for you, it's more useful than a fossil-fuel truck because it can do stuff that fossil fuel trucks can't do, and it solves problems that you have with your old fossil-fuel truck, like purchasing gas with rising oil prices or constant maintenance. Ford flips the conversation from "here is an environmentally conscious choice that is also functional" to "here is a product that is incredibly functional and also environmentally conscious." Lowered greenhouse gas emissions are not the focus but merely a happy coincidence.

FOR THE ADVANCED (CAR-LOVING) READER

Ford reports that the truck can go from zero to sixty MPH in just over four seconds, operate for 240 miles on a single charge, can charge at your home overnight, and tow nearly eight thousand pounds. It also has a fifteen-inch touch screen mounted to the dash that gives the driver complete control over the vehicle and extra exterior lights to illuminate worksites at night.[71]

---

71 "2023 Ford® F-150 Lightning Electric Truck: All Electric and All F-150," Ford Motor Company, accessed November 1, 2022, https://www.ford.com/trucks/f150/f150-lightning/.

Actually the F-150 Lightning is beyond functional. Here's the really genius thing: the F-150 Lightning can be used as a mobile generator. If you drive a Ford Lightning, your truck can power your house if there is a power outage or power an off-grid jobsite (made possible because the car is electric). Again, rather than thinking of building an electric car because it would be better for the environment, Ford thought of utilitarian reasons for building an electric car: It can do more stuff. In the same way that smartphones transformed the consumer's relationship with the phone from a single function (to make calls) to an essential life assistant, the Ford F-150 Lightning is looking to transcend vehicles from their singular duty of getting people from one location to another.

THEY AREN'T ALL WINS

We also need to admit that all attempts at making products that would be better for the environment did not work. For example, low-flow toilets. They seemed like a good idea, and everybody got one. And then they flushed and discovered: low-flow toilets frequently don't flush all the way. So you flush twice or three times or seven times, and therefore in actual use, the product negates the concept that would have made it more water efficient—you've used more water than you would have with a regular toilet.

Low-flow showerheads have a similar issue: not enough water comes out to rinse off the soap, so what do you do? Take a longer shower. Again, the way the consumer uses the product negates the environmental benefit.

These products, and others like them, were created and marketed in good faith but didn't work. We need to recognize that while the innovation was correct, these particular ideas were not successful. Only by realizing what worked and what did not can we work toward successful innovations.

Lightning is an essential, multifunctional tool. Both the product and the PR behind it brilliantly assessed the market, filled a need, and presented the product in a way that, in the end, related not only to working-class truck drivers—their practical approach marketing appealed to consumers up and down the socioeconomic chain. The monologue at the end of the advertisement says, "It's about towing, hauling, powering a campsite or worksite ... the only EV built Ford tough. The only EV smart enough, fast enough to carry our name."

LET'S COUNT THE (MORE THAN) TRIPLE WIN

1. Don't have to buy gas

2. Spend far less on maintenance (no engine, no oil change, etc.)

3. Works as a generator

4. Lowers your carbon footprint

5. Worried about the time it will take to charge? You can now charge from anywhere that has access to electricity, which means you can plug in while you are at home, at the grocery store, at work, etc. rather than standing outside at the pump.

Then the announcer modifies his original question, "Can *this* truck change everything?"[72] As I write this book at the end of 2022, the header on Ford's official website for the 2023 Lightning reads: "Due to high demand, the current model year is no longer available for retail order."[73]

Products like the Ford Lightning take the conflict out of the conversation. They are not initiating debate about whether or not climate

---

72   Ibid.

73   Ibid.

change is real or whether we should do something about it; instead, they are focused on giving consumers what they want. In Oklahoma, when I talk to neighboring farmers about Ford's new F-150, we talk about how great it would be to have those bright spotlights so that we could see a fence we're mending in the middle of the night or how sick we are of our current gas vehicles breaking down. Our conversations about regenerative farming are similar. We aren't debating whether or not the climate is changing but talking about how to increase yields and decrease risks. These are pragmatic rather than philosophical conversations. Not only can we agree on what we want, but our conversations lead to action.

How to Train Horses

When potential employees interview for positions in one of my organizations, I often ask them: What do you think is the difference between manipulation and influence? Most people intrinsically know that manipulation is different from influence because manipulation has something to do with screwing someone over, whereas influence is a suggestion. I break it down like this: Manipulation is when you are driving someone's behavior to get something you want; influence is when you are on driving someone's behavior to get what he or she wants. I want to use psychological constructs to inform, educate, and influence, not to manipulate. People do not like to be controlled. They prefer freedom, independence, and choice. When people act out of that freedom and independence, their actions are more sustainable.

Manipulation is often secretive and sneaky, whereas influence can be very upfront. Influence is also related to trust, openness, and a willingness to reveal what's behind the curtain. The influencer can announce, and I frequently do, "I'm trying to help you do this," and give the person who is being influenced a peek behind the curtain.

"Look, this is what I'm encouraging you to do, here's why, and let me explain the strategy I am using to do so." I like to be direct in this way.

When I used to train horses, I practiced a version of natural horsemanship where the trainer strives to make her idea the horse's idea rather than constantly imposing commands (followed by reward and punishment) on the horse. It is considered a kinder and gentler form of training based on psychology. You don't need a bridal. You don't need a halter. You don't need a saddle. You don't need anything except communication with the horse. The trainer and horse get to know one another, and the horse learns to feel what the rider is thinking in a way. After months of training, my horse, Sandy, could sense my weight shifting in the saddle and knew that I wanted to speed up or slow down; she could feel my head turn to look in a particular direction and knew which way I wanted to go. I didn't have to say or do a thing. By the time she died, we could basically read one another's minds. My ideas were Sandy's ideas, and probably vice versa.

SOME DEFINITIONS

The Merriam-Webster definition (not required for a correct answer) of manipulation is, "to control or play upon by artful, unfair, or insidious means especially to one's own advantage"[74] Influence is defined as having "an effect on the condition or development."[75]

I worked as a horse trainer for a while in the Bay Area where I helped wealthy horse owners develop relationships with their horses (so that their horses could read their minds too). I used to tell them

74   Influence Definition & Meaning." Merriam-Webster, Merriam-Webster, https://www.merriam-webster.com/dictionary/influence.

75   Manipulation Definition & Meaning." Merriam-Webster, Merriam-Webster, https://www.merriam-webster.com/dictionary/manipulation.

they would know they had a good relationship with their horse when they could shower together and turn to rinse off without bumping one another. The goal of the training was that both the rider and the horse were in tune with one another's thoughts and desires enough to predict movement and behavior.

TIGHT SPACES

One day I was out riding Sandy, and I had to go to the bathroom really badly. I was in a park that was pretty public and couldn't leave her outside, so I brought her into the women's restroom. This, of course, was not a situation to which she was accustomed, and the women's restroom was also not accustomed to accommodating horses. It was one of those one-person, cramped situations with the toilet and sink locked like puzzle pieces. Sandy and I were packed into the space. The whole situation was not ideal.

"Just hang, baby. Just be cool," I assured her, and quickly did my business.

Things were fine until it was time to leave. Sandy obviously couldn't turn around in there. I needed to back her out. When I moved to open the door, she looked up and caught a glimpse of her own reflection in the mirror.

I'm pretty certain she thought, "Oh shit. There's another horse in here. A very fine-looking horse, but how the hell did she get in here?"

There was a moment when we both panicked. Sandy about the other horse, me about how Sandy was going to react in the tight space.

"It's cool," I was saying, guiding her toward the open door.

She backed up, believing me, still tracking the other horse who had the same desire to just get the hell out of there.

I'M NOT SAYING PEOPLE ARE HORSES (EXACTLY)

My knowledge of horse training has come in very handy when trying to inspire people to behave differently. Because people find it disparaging to be compared to animals ("I'm not a horse," "I wasn't born in a barn," "I'm a brilliant, God-ordained human," yada yada ...), they often don't like this comparison, so I'm not officially making it, but off the record, encouraging people to behave differently is like training horses. I often look at a negative pattern of behavior in an organization or community that needs to change and think to myself, I've got to train some horses.

Like training a horse, inspiring someone to adopt new behavior works best when you make a suggestion that the person adopts as his or her own idea. In order to do this, you must first relate to the individual and understand what drives him or her. What does she want? Then you can think of ways to motivate a new behavior based on feeding that desire.

Regardless of socioeconomic levels, everyone wants something. People are basic in this way. There are two basic motivators that guide people: greed and ego. There is the person who feels better knowing he or she is not hurting the planet or is concerned about his or her legacy, ego, and the person who is focused on what they get out of a situation or who wants to buck the system (I definitely fall into this camp sometimes), greed. Both of these worldviews are selfish, meaning people are generally self-focused. On top of this, people want to do what is easy (this is especially true now when humans as an entity on the planet are so comparatively prosperous).

I don't say this as a judgment of human beings (although I have my opinions), I say this as a way of strategizing how to talk to people and motivate them to take action. Think of advertising slogans like

"More for less," "Be the first," "You have the power to make change," and "Save time." People relate to messages that essentially say: This will make life easier for you, you're going to get something out of this, or this will make you look good or feel good about yourself. These are the things that make us happy.

I drive a Tesla. Most people probably own a Tesla either because they are wealthy CEOs and see it as a status symbol or because it's a high-performance vehicle that's awesome to drive. Looking cool and going fast are not what drive me. I bought a Tesla because it has enough room for my kids, their baseball gear, art projects, all their other nonsense, and the groceries—I'm a mom, and cargo space is essential for my life. The Tesla fits my life in other ways: It's practical— the car can be charged to easily power my one-hour commute to work, and it satisfies my ego, allowing me to feel I am doing my part to lower greenhouse gas emissions.

I have friends who have different motivations for owning electric and hybrid cars. Several of my friends with hybrid cars like to game the system by getting around town without using gas. They do things like changing gears while going downhill or staying at an exact speed limit in order to regenerate energy and continue to use the battery. Some go as far as to engineer routes that will be more fuel efficient.

In order to encourage people to act in more environmentally conscious ways, you must first know your horses: what they desire and what will motivate them. What motivates Bill Gates (who is environmentally conscious) will be different from what motivates Warren Buffet (who doesn't believe ESG has a future). Both want something. If you can understand what that is, you can begin to offer options or information that appeal to their particular desires.

What does Bill Gates care about? Legacy? Good PR? Environment? Making smart business decisions? Building and maintaining businesses? When I fully understand this, I can find a way to motivate him by framing the argument and leading him to something he wants without taking anything away from him. I can offer him the information he wants, give him options for how he can use that information to get more of what he wants, appeal to his desire for greed or ego, and influence him to act. I don't want to manipulate him. I want him to choose to take action because he wants to do so. If I am trying to encourage Warren Buffet, I'm going to do all of these same things. I'm going to start by trying to understand what he cares about and wants, then work to appeal those desires. Those conversations and appeals will obviously need to very different, but in the end, they can result in similar behavior. People often do the same things for very different reasons.

Ideally this works like a well-oiled machine. People are encouraged to change their behavior based on appeals to their specific desires. Changing their behavior should be easy and rewarding for them. It often does not require that they do something entirely new, but that they direct their current actions with a new intention. This new action benefits both them and the environment, and they continue to do it either out of greed (what am I getting out of it) or ego (this makes me feel good about myself). Everybody wins.

I want to push beyond even the influencing when encouraging people's behavior. I invented the term "pro-climate impactor," which is different from the term a lot of people use: pro-climate influencer. First of all, the term influencer is associated with celebrities made famous on TikTok or Instagram for espousing life lessons about applying makeup. That's just not what we're about. Influence refers to the ability to persuade others without exerting force or issuing an explicit command. To impact means to make a deep impression—like the meteor that impacted the earth and killed most of the dinosaurs. An impact does not merely persuade someone to change their behavior, it is so significant as to affect somebody's mindset or life trajectory. That's what I want to do. Influencers talk; impactors act. I have focused my companies on measurable and tangible actions that have lasting effects. People in business are uniquely situated to have an impact through outreach. We have access to a mass of people and the big brains and big mouths that we need to inform, educate, inspire, and take action.

In order to make an impact, my consultants also need to be the chefs and not the waiters. Waiters help facilitate the experience of the meal, but the chef creates the food and the experience. I want my consultants to assume the chef role with our clients. The same way a master chef brings together experience, knowledge, and passion to combine ingredients and craft an unforgettable culinary experience for patrons, I want my employees to create the experience that incites the commitment, emotion, and inspiration that impels clients to continue to hire us and to maintain their ESG efforts. We need to earn our place in this conversation by bringing our long hours of research and analysis, as well as our compassion and empathy to the equation.

BEST CHEF CREATION

This onion truffle-thing I ate in Florence. I didn't know I needed it, but now that I have experienced it fully, I am forever changed.

Show Them and They'll Be All Ears

I needed to have a water well drilled in Oklahoma. The well guy came out, and we had the same conversation that I have had with everyone in Oklahoma. "You from California? You must be here to farm pot. I guess you probably hate Trump, huh?" Then we got down to business. He started talking about groundwater and what was feasible in terms of the geology of the area. The issue was that I needed a well that would be sufficient for irrigating a farm of my size. "Tell me about your farm," he said. "What are you going to use the irrigation for?"

I started talking crops.

"I read a little something about your nonprofit," he told me. It ended up that Dr. Tatiana had mentioned it to him when she'd called and asked him to come out. "I don't understand what you're trying to do here," he said.

I explained the regenerative farming concept and how ultimately regenerative farms are a way to enact drawdown, which is an answer to climate change—those words came out of my mouth, "climate change."

He did not bristle immediately. He said, "Well, that's interesting." Then he said, "You know, there's a lot of people around here who don't believe in climate change."

"Yeah, I know," I said. "I'm okay with that." And I genuinely was. I'm not trying to convert beliefs; I'm trying to change behavior. I massage the conversation so that the well guy did not feel threatened, working my way back to crops and aquifers.

When he was convinced that I truly did not care what he believed, he said, "I am one of those people. I don't believe in climate change. I've lived here all my life, for forty-six years, I've seen extreme weather here for decades. My parents saw that before me, and my grandparents before that. We are a place of extreme weather."

I nodded. "I agree with you," I said, and I shifted the conversation away from the larger concept of climate change and toward the tangible things that I thought we could agree on. "But maybe we can also agree that the farming industry is dying. If you've been here for so long, maybe you've seen that it's impossible to make a living as a farmer here now. Wouldn't it be awesome if we could get more moisture in the soil?" This was his department after all.

People are often talking about the same things with different words; offended by particular terms and accepting of others that mean the same thing. Part of learning to connect is simply changing our vocabulary. Many of the terms that we use to describe environmentally conscious solutions sound complicated, expensive, or gross. No wonder they are not appealing. We need to use terms that sound the opposite.

"Gray water system" for example sounds suspicious as hell. No one wants the word "gray" attached to their water (dirty, gray-area, etc.), and "systems" sounds complicated, like something you definitely need to hire a few professionals to deal with. A gray water system simply means diverting water from your bath or laundry (not the toilet) into irrigation. We could call it "washing machine flower-watering pipe," "recycled watering," or the gamified version, "Tomato Deal Water." The marketing strategy for "recycled watering" could simply be that while water prices are on the rise, the consumer can save money and have a beautiful yard! And it's easy. You don't have to use special shampoos or chemically treat the water before it gets dumped on your tomatoes. You just hook up your pipe, take your shower, and grow your garden. Changing our vocabulary can be a part of shifting the conversation. We can use terms that stress how actions and products are good for consumers—efficient, cheap, etc.

I started talking about the farming side of what I was doing. Not only do we need new words, but we need an entire shift in the conversation, away from theory and philosophy and toward things that are practical, tangible, and actionable. I spoke about our past harvest at Rainmaker Farm, the actions we were taking, the difficult farming decisions that I was making. All of this he understood. I talked about the difficult position where farmers found themselves, not wanting to spray herbicides, but finding they had to spray in order to preserve their crop, and how expensive it was to spray. Now I was speaking his language, and the conversation took off.

Then we started digging into regenerative farming concepts, but rather than using words like "regenerative farming," "sustainability," or even "carbon," we talked water, moisture, and irrigation. He could agree that retaining more moisture in the soil and protecting aquifers would be absolutely beneficial for the farming community. He could also agree that, through traditional farming methods, it simply was not possible. We talked about water tables, irrigation, and rainfall. All of these things that are part of the ecosystem being affected by climate change and which my practices of regenerative farming are working to improve. Like me, he wanted better soil that was more effective for growing crops so that farmers could have a more consistent, lucrative way of life. He agreed that it would be good to find a way to farm that would be better for the farming community and ultimately better for the ground, which is better for the earth. That's what I am doing at Rainmaker Farm. In the end, he supported the practices of regenerative farming, although he still rejected the term "climate change." We were on the same page.

Many of my conversations about climate change and regenerative farming have happened this way. And still more have not happened at all. I prefer to communicate by example. I want to show rather than preach. Rainmaker Farm demonstrates the ideas of regenerative farming and allows me to be part of the conversation through my actions. Rather than being in a fight about climate change or the merits of regenerative farming, people will see the success of my farm. Another farmer once said to me, "There ain't no farmer out here who's going to listen to you if you're talking. But if you show them, if you have an example, then they're going to be all ears."

The well guy went on to tell me about his life. He was a missionary who had traveled the world and had many experiences. When he left, he shook my hand and said, "I've really truly enjoyed this conversation, and I'm excited to come and talk to you again." He didn't say that as a polite exit, it was genuine. Before he left, he said something that I had been thinking, "You know, we're so much more the same than we are different."

SIMILAR SOLUTIONS

It turns out that there wasn't groundwater available on my parcel (which is common and why many people in this region rely on rural water networks). When the well guy called to inform me that the exploratory drilling came up dry, he mentioned that many of the old-timers did water catchment, just like the system I'd developed at my off-the-grid house in California. I could apply the same strategy to my Oklahoma farm.

Take Action: Come Together, Right Now

Being successful in implementing changes with meaningful positive impacts on the environment requires mass participation. That means people from disparate backgrounds and with a range of ideas and experiences need to be motivated to work together. In order to organize and inspire people to achieve a united goal, you must first find a way to communicate effectively—in a way that can be heard and accepted by many. Listen. Be humble. Be open. Train your horses.

Tier 1: The Savvy At-Home Composter

1. Start a grassroots environmentally conscious initiative about something you are passionate about. Grassroots organizing can have a major impact on local areas and can develop into large initiatives. These actions help communities connect.

2. Use social media to develop local communication networks that keep people connected and informed about the various concerns and perspectives in your area.

Tier 2: The CEO Environmental Powerhouse

1. Think of yourself as part of a larger community. Turning the conference rooms, where you currently train your employees, into workforce development centers for your community is only a matter of scheduling.

2. Create formal and informal forums where employees and people in your community can express concerns and learn from one another.

3. Teach your employees and communities how to maintain, deploy, and speak about the green tech that you champion.

4. Do all the stuff the Savvy At-Home Composter is doing.

Tier 3: The Big Cheese World Changer

1. Participate in panels, conferences, interviews, and other opportunities that allow you to communicate with those in and outside of your industry.

2. Create connections between disparate communities through initiatives, events, or new networks.

3. Do all the stuff the CEO Environmental Powerhouse is doing.

4. Do all the stuff the Savvy At-Home Composter is doing.

Bringing Sexy Back

Starting Rainmaker Farm is one of the most tangible things that I've done to help the environment, and I've learned a lot from the endeavor. It solidified a lot of my beliefs about people, how to affect real change, and the many benefits of really walking my talk when it comes to being environmentally conscious. Rainmaker Farm is a big project that cost money and time but has far more than paid off on my investment, and it will continue to pay going into the future.

Rainmaker Farm gave me access to another world and people who think differently than the CEOs I affiliate with at conferences, clients I work with, or San Francisco Bay Area neighbors I occasionally see. The farmers in the area have different concerns and a different understanding and approach to issues. But what is truly enlightening is not the difference in our perspectives, but upon how much we agree. Even the Beethoven of Bees, who to this day has nothing nice to say about my newfangled Flow Hives, knows that the regenerative farm model produces healthier soil and allows farmers to be better stewards of the land. Rainmaker Farm has started a revolution, showing that a return to regenerative farming is possible, and most importantly starting a conversation between two ideologies that seem divided but in fact want the same things.

There is no end to the conversations that Rainmaker Farm has started. Whenever and wherever I mention it, people are interested: CEOs who have never stepped foot in a field, people across all industries, waitresses at airport restaurants all lean in to hear me tell stories about adventures and misadventures in Oklahoma (experience has given me a lot of stories). They like to hear about the farm because it is not just a theory, it is an actual place shaped by physical work, and there are cows (who doesn't like cows). My association with a farm is something unexpected that most would not imagine was possible (a CEO starting a farm is a premise for a sitcom, *Green Acres*), but there it is. The very existence of the farm is hopeful; its success is invigorating. Stories of the farm can transform any conversation into one centered on environmentalism, away from disagreement about philosophies, and toward the generation of ideas and plans for action that we can all agree upon.

A NOTE FROM DR. TATIANA

It is very controversial to say you are doing something environmentally conscious incorporating cattle. Cattle are often considered environmental enemy #1. They can have detrimental impacts on the environment ranging from decreasing water quality to generating greenhouse gases. Limiting the number of cattle globally is the main focus of many environmental campaigns.[76] That being said, like with any land management, there are a range of possible environmental outcomes from different land management practices, including within cattle grazing. The Audubon Society even recognizes ranchers who manage their land in a way that is beneficial to native birds through their Conservation Ranching Program.

From a business standpoint, the inspiration generated through conversations about Rainmaker Farm translates into opportunity. It means that people are spreading the word about me and my companies, they are wanting to be involved, and they are seeking out partnerships and relationships with my businesses. The farm has produced, as a by-product, possibilities for all kinds of marketing.

---

76 A. Quinton, "Cows and Climate Change," UC Davis, June 27, 2019, https://www.ucdavis.edu/food/news/making-cattle-more-sustainable.

What the farm made obvious to me, and to everyone who learned about it, is that anything is possible. Anyone can do this. It wasn't an amazing accomplishment; I did what most entrepreneurs do every day. I saw an opportunity, found a way, learned as I went, and fearlessly jumped in.

POTENTIAL AD: RAINMAKER FARM BUSINESS RETREATS

Poster Ad: Picture of Rainmaker Farm looking especially fabulous

Copy: Rainmaker Farm Business Retreats: Coming Soon! (Possibly)

Grow together through business retreats and team-building activities with an environmental focus at Rainmaker Farm.

Also included: wine, snacks, cornhole.

There are countless benefits for taking environmentally conscious actions; the cost of not doing so is to become obsolete. Now is the time to be on the forefront of the evolving ecological economy. This is the ESG wave. Waves are tricky to ride, but a good ride is well worth the effort—exhilarating, awesome, and a chance to show off your skills and be a part of the conversation. Don't miss the wave. Those who realize too late that the surf is good will be left behind. Figure out how you—as a business owner or employee or person at home—can capitalize on your own resourcefulness to get (more than) a triple win: act in a more environmentally conscious way (save the planet, feel great about yourself, look good, save money),

A FINAL NOTE FROM DR. TATIANA

It is infuriating to me that through this book "triple win" almost never meant "three ways." "Triple" means "three" not four, or five ...

market those actions (create products and services), and grow your business or investment (reach a larger clientele, make a name for yourself as an industry leader).

In November of 2022, I was invited to the WE3 Summit to be on a panel titled "The Bold Net-Zero Utilities." I gave a keynote speech before my panel discussion. Before I got on stage, the stage manager said, "I know we told you that you'd have fifteen minutes, but you've only got four. Here's the mic." It was a moment that felt very typical of my life in business and as a pro-climate impactor. Things were always shifting, and I was always shifting my weight right along with them. I jumped on stage ready to go. I wanted to make an impact.

Everyone at the conference had already been given a copy of the Decarbonization Report. I started my talk by briefly telling them who I was and why I had been invited to speak. After twenty years of working in the utility industry, I had taken it upon myself to create the NPUC, which over the past two years had identified five barriers that utilities face to reaching net-zero greenhouse gas emissions. Then I essentially said, "We already know the barriers, and here they are." I listed them. "I don't want to talk to you about barriers anymore," I said. "I want to talk to you about the solutions that you can use right now." Then I told the audience that they could skip my panel, call their assistants, and get started on implementing those solutions immediately.

Don't get me wrong, conversation and communication are essential. But as industry leaders, governments, scientists, and community members, we've done a lot of that. I spent months in meetings with the NPUC members talking about issues and challenges, which was critical to understanding what we needed to do to progress. In most industries, people have been talking about ESG issues and identifying barriers similarly. Now it's time to shift the conversation toward solutions and actions.

For those of the audience who stayed (rather than jumping up to implement the solutions I'd suggested), which unfortunately was most of them, I used my remaining minute to shift the conversation. "We're bringing sexy back to utilities," I told them. "Do you guys believe me? Look at these pants."[77] I was wearing black pants with an elegant flower print that stood in stark contrast to the sea of gray business suits worn by almost everyone in attendance and, I must say, looked damn good. The audience laughed.

A Picture of My Pants

When I say that I want to bring sexy back, I mean that I want to bring back innovation and excitement. Talking over and over about problems is not exciting. Trying new things is exciting. Doing things is exciting. Nothing is sexier than an innovative solution in action.

I want industries, CEOs, and all humans to understand their power to get the world to net-zero greenhouse gas emissions and beyond. I want them to embody a new perspective of leadership and

---

77 YouTube, "WE3 2022: The Bold Net-Zero Utilities," YouTube, retrieved December 1, 2022, from https://www.youtube.com/watch?v=6MmoU1544W4.

ingenuity. "Let's talk about how utilities are now on the hook to revolutionize our society," I said to the audience. "Let's revolutionize utilities. If we do this, we will be the next Google. We will be the next Microsoft. If we can become the matrix to a revolutionary solution, then we will become sexy. We will attract all the young people to come and work for us. We will drive innovation. We will drive technology. We will drive the public private partnership that we must develop in order to move forward. We will drive workforce development and community elevation across the board. This is not a pipe dream. It is practical; it is tangible. And I have answers to how we do it. Maybe not all of them, but I have a lot of them. Let's talk about those tangible actions. Let's talk about what you're going to do going forward."[78]

Many utilities who are members of the NPUC are already taking action. Duke Energy, for example, is trying to solve the problem of managing low-rate structures for disadvantaged communities. After talking about the issue and solutions in a roundtable with other participants of the NPUC, they decided to have a fixed-fee rate structure. You do this by regulating heat management practices, which means that you need to install digital thermostats, maintain those thermostats, and make sure that everyone in the community has internet access—an added bonus and significant win for people in that community.

Duke Energy realized that in order to enact their plan, they were going to need to connect with industries outside of utilities. They were thinking outside the box. They found a program through Honeywell for deploying digital thermostats to disadvantaged communities. Next they contacted an internet provider (AT&T) that had a program for low-income customers and worked together with the provider to create a service bundle so that Duke Energy customers would have

---

78   Ibid.

free internet access. Duke Energy united three companies to enact a solution that drives carbon dioxide emissions down, regulates usage, is available for an economically disadvantaged community, and involves the community in the process.

MY RANT ABOUT BUSINESS SUITS

I recently swore off business suits. Fuck business suits. I hate them. You're trying to be taken seriously by dressing the part rather than acting the part and having people pay attention because of your mind. I spent twenty years in boxy man-suits effectively trying to fit in and not be overtly female among mostly male CEOs. When I was pregnant, I had business suits for maternity that tried to diminish the visibility of my pregnancy. It's too contrived for me.

I'm almost fifty years old, and I refuse to keep playing that game simply because it is what is done, or what has been done for decades. I'm walking my talk and thinking outside the box in innovative ways when it comes to dressing for conferences, even those attended by everyone from the CEO of TikTok to Carl Rove with Leslie Stall from 60 Minutes set up to interview people, which was the scene. It has been a very liberating experience.

I first disrupted the traditional fashion scene at the YPO Conference in New York (where everything is about fashion) where I had to deliver a keynote speech. I wore orange velvet pants. It was awesome. What I didn't know was that on the main stage, there were black lights everywhere. When I walked on stage, my pants turned an electric, rock-star pink. They looked nuclear.

Seattle City Light, another participant of the NPUC, also successfully implemented changes by capitalizing on existing outreach initiatives. They identified a problem with existing outreach efforts: Utilities were asking the community the wrong questions because they did not fully understand those communities. They started employing people from those communities to be liaisons in the existing town halls. The next time they asked the communities, "What can we do to better serve you? Offer lower rate structures, different peak times, different devices like LED light bulbs or access to different resources?" The community liaisons stood up and said, "Yes, we'd love all those things, but what we really need is light in bus stops because most of us commute at night, and the bus stops are dark and therefore dangerous. It would be really helpful if you, as the utility, could run electricity to bus stops."

Seattle City Light had not considered bus stops before that town hall, but with their new communication methods in place, they had access to their customer base, could learn about the real issues their customers faced, and could solve those issues.

And there are all kinds of sexy ways to solve issues. Think about the Ford F-150 Lightning that can power a worksite or Duke Energy getting internet service for all of their customers. Think about a triple win. Think about your company becoming the thought leader in a particular area or industry by creating an innovative solution. This is a challenge and also an opportunity.

There are many ways to catch the wave and become part of the environmentally conscious movement. You could start a farm, or you could support regenerative farming. You could start a garden or implement a composting or recycling program at work or in a local community. You could install solar panels, plant trees, find a more energy efficient way to commute, or institute programs that help to do any of these on a large scale. You could learn and educate others about becoming more environmentally conscious. You could look at your current interests and actions through an ecological lens, try new things, get together with a diverse group of people to talk about solving problems. You could work on getting yourself, your business, or your community to net-zero greenhouse gas emissions. You could vote for environmentally beneficial initiatives. You could use your purchasing power to support environmentally conscious or ESG compliant companies. You could promote all the good environmental choices that you make by telling a friend, writing a post, wearing a T-shirt with the logo of your awesome new foundation. By walking your talk in any of these ways, you too will create inspirational experiences like those I created at Rainmaker Farm. You will make connections with other people and businesses. You will generate opportunities.

Join the movement for a greener future! Discover our family of companies, united by a shared commitment to sustainability and equipped with vast resources and innovative insights. Together we navigate the complexities of driving a more environmentally responsible future.

Motive Power

Empower your organization with tailored ESG solutions from Motive Power. Scan to learn how we can help you lead the way!

10/6 Professional Services

Drive your projects to success with 10/6's expert-driven approach. Scan to learn about our commitment to sustainable project management!

National Public Utilities Council (NPUC)

Join NPUC's journey in revolutionizing the energy sector. Scan to gain insights into collaborative efforts and research driving us towards a decarbonized future.

The National Public Utilities Council – Decarbonization Channel

Discover the US energy sector's path to decarbonization through compelling data-driven infographics and visualizations. Scan for captivating insights.

The National Public Utilities Council – Annual Utility Decarbonization Report

Dive into our Annual Utility Decarbonization Report to uncover the challenges utilities face and the innovative solutions propelling the shift to greener energy. Download now for a clearer path to decarbonization!

The Gulch Environmental Foundation

Make an impact today! Scan to explore how you can help drive progress in solving the climate crisis through carbon sequestration.

The Gulch Environmental Foundation – Donate Today

Donate today and empower change! Be a part of the solution by supporting our work in combating climate change through carbon sequestration projects. Scan to donate and make a difference!

DONATE TODAY!

ACKNOWLEDGMENTS

There are various people who played important roles on the journey of the creation of this book. Two stand out most particularly: my dear scientist friend and research partner in environmental crime Aviva Rossi, who, through much coffee and conversation, helped shift my mind toward action in the environmental space; the good people of my companies who help drive action in this mission every day; and lastly Dana Kroos, a pure delight to work with on the fine craft of authoring. Her humor and mental availability made this process more pleasurable than I thought possible.

ABOUT THE AUTHOR

ANGEL LANCE is an active entrepreneur of businesses spanning management consulting, real estate, and agriculture. Her mission is to use her skills (and acquire new ones along the way) to bridge the gaps in human understanding and awareness of humanity itself and its environment (physical and social). Angel is the mother of two children, a boy and a girl, and lives in the greater San Francisco Bay Area.

Printed in the USA
CPSIA information can be obtained
at www.ICGtesting.com
JSHW021104211223
54170JS00007B/14/J